D0122316

THE FARM
ON THE ROOF

THE FARM
ON THE ROOF

WHAT BROOKLYN GRANGE
TAUGHT US ABOUT
ENTREPRENEURSHIP,
COMMUNITY, AND GROWING
A SUSTAINABLE BUSINESS

ANASTASIA COLE PLAKIAS

AVERY   AN IMPRINT OF PENGUIN RANDOM HOUSE   NEW YORK

AVERY

an imprint of Penguin Random House LLC
375 Hudson Street
New York, New York 10014

Most Avery books are available at special quantity discounts for
bulk purchase for sales promotions, premiums, fund-raising,
and educational needs. Special books or book excerpts also
can be created to fit specific needs. For details, write
SpecialMarkets@penguinrandomhouse.com.

ISBN: 978-1-59240-948-8

Printed in the United States of America
1 3 5 7 9 10 8 6 4 2

BOOK DESIGN BY MEIGHAN CAVANAUGH

To our amazing farmily who gave us a hand along the way. To the moms and dads who believed in us; the friends who listened and helped us solve problems; the investors, lenders, and Kickstarter supporters who put their money where their mouths were; the neighborhood green thumbs; the experienced farmers who picked up our calls; the girlfriends and boyfriends who cooked us dinners when we came home late; the husbands and wives who took an extra morning shift so we could get to work early; the journalists who helped us spread the word; the lawyers who gave us free advice; the coffee shops that gave us free Wi-Fi ... There are too many to mention everyone by name, but we can never give thanks enough to the folks who've shown up in blasting heat and howling winds to make sure Brooklyn Grange thrives: Hester, Rob, Michael, Melissa, Michele, Matt, Bradley, Alia, Robyn, Cashen, and Tori, we love you.

CONTENTS

THE FARM
ON THE ROOF

Introduction

NOWHERE TO GO BUT UP

As 2008 rolled in, New York City was riding high: the economy was up, the crime rate was down, and something in the air made it feel like the greatest city in the world, at the greatest time in its history. The seedy Times Square of yesteryear had turned into Disneyland. Once-blighted areas of Brooklyn were reinventing themselves as meccas of creativity. Sidewalk cafés were teeming with urban sophisticates drinking three-dollar lattes. Tourists streamed in and out of attractions, buying tchotchkes from street vendors. Some complained that this town wasn't gritty enough, but nobody seemed to mind that they could take the subway home late at night without fearing for their safety, iPhone earbuds tucked blithely into their ears.

Then in September of that year, everything fell apart: the

subprime mortgage crisis, banking bust, and auto industry implosion triggered an economic downturn that had newspaper headlines warning of the next great depression. As the largest regional economy in the United States, New York City took the hit, hard. Sure, it could have been worse. New York wasn't Detroit, and the city remained relatively prosperous. But the shift was palpable. Suddenly the spirit of consumption that had defined the prior decade seemed embarrassingly ostentatious.

On TV screens across the country, a woman named Sarah Palin warned Main Street about the corporate cronyism of Wall Street. Meanwhile, a Black man was running for president on a platform of change and making young voters believe it was something they had the power to effect. The nation was at a crossroads: On the one hand, our sense of security had been dashed and everything we thought we knew about being the most powerful country in the world was revealed to be the long con of a powerful few. On the other hand, as this reality dawned, it brought with it the prospect of a new day. As voters streamed into polling precincts at the highest rates in forty years, one thing became clear: the country believed in hope.

This was the climate in which we—myself and a handful of other scrappy young Brooklynites—first came together to start Brooklyn Grange, the world's first commercial rooftop farm.

Each of us left behind promising careers during the worst recession in decades to do something about which we were totally uncertain. It wasn't that we had doubts about urban farming—urban farms had existed long before we decided to start one. And while no one had ever practiced rooftop farming at the scale we set out to, humans had succeeded in growing plants on roofs since the fabled hanging gardens of Babylon. But we set out to do it differently. We didn't simply want to farm; we intended to create a small farm *business*—a self-sustaining enterprise that, like any other business, would have to turn a profit to survive. In an industry as fickle, susceptible, and lean as farming—and in an economic climate as competitive as the one in which we found ourselves—success was not a given.

If you're thinking that we started this endeavor because we saw an easy path to success, think again. Even though we're now thriving, we will never be millionaires doing what we do, nor will we ever spend our summers on a shady porch sipping lemonade. Running our farm the way we do was important for other reasons. Led by our entrepreneurial head farmer and president, Ben Flanner, myself, and my partner Gwen Schantz, along with the owners of Roberta's, a Brooklyn pizzeria, and later joined by our partner Chase Emmons, we were determined to operate a for-profit enterprise growing vegetables on a roof because we wanted to prove it was a worthwhile endeavor. By operating it as a for-profit enterprise, we set out to show the

wider world that urban farming can be both an agricultur-
ally and fiscally sustainable operation—an industry that, if invested in, could help change the landscape of cities.

We also knew there was a long list of very good reasons that
no one had ever done this before. Agriculture requires a certain
scale to be profitable, and land in cities is scarce and expensive. And while rooftop space is less valuable than ground-level
real estate, the cost of building it out is higher. What's more, we
were determined to be a *truly* sustainable business, focused not
just on numbers but on what is known as the triple bottom
line. Business authority John Eklington developed the triple-
bottom-line framework to describe a business that accounts for
its performance across three categories known as the Three Ps:
people, planet, and profit. If a corporation generates revenues by
pillaging an ecosystem of its resources, it is deriving profits at
the expense of the planet. If another business manages to make
a profit without wreaking ecological damage but must lay off
an entire community of workers in order to do so, its benefits
to the planet are coming at the cost of the people who inhabit
it. The idea is to derive revenues while also generating natural
and human capital: everybody wins.

We had set out to create not only a financial return from our
rooftop farm but a social and ecological return as well. There
were times early on when it seemed like we'd bitten off more
than we could chew, and even now, we still have a long road

and many uphill climbs ahead of us before our business achieves the myriad goals we've set out to tackle. But five years after rolling out the first layer of green roof atop our flagship farm, we're operating two and a half acres on two buildings in Brooklyn and Queens, we manage more than thirty beehives across the city, and we've built acres of urban green space for partner organizations and private clients. We've raised more than a million dollars between two rounds of fund-raising, and have built a team of eleven full-time staff as well as a network of partner organizations who help make our rooftops a learning laboratory and refuge for students, immigrants, and other New Yorkers.

Still, when we were approached to write this book, we were thrown for a bit of a loop. We'd talked about a book for a while, but we weren't quite sure what it would look like. There's a whole canon of credible literature on sustainable farming out there, and our forefarmers, such as Eliot Coleman, who pioneered many of the techniques we use on our farm, describe our growing methods better than we ever could. Richard Wiswall's *The Organic Farmer's Business Handbook* delves into the importance of accounting in order to farm profitably. Lauren Mandel's *Eat Up: The Inside Scoop on Rooftop Agriculture* does a nice job of discussing different green roof configurations and installation methods, and Annie Novak, our friend and colleague right here in New York City, recently penned the ultimate compendium, *The Rooftop Growing Guide: How to Transform Your Roof into a Vegetable Garden or Farm.* So what the heck did we have to contribute to the genre?

Then our editor suggested we write a business book. At first, we were skeptical. We'd only been around for a few years, after all, and had just eleven full-time staff. We didn't start paying dividends until the end of 2014, four years into operating. Surely others were more qualified to write about launching a commercial enterprise. Ultimately, though, we realized the story we wanted to tell really was about business. It was about striving to achieve the triple-bottom-line model we aspired to, and we figured our story about planning, building, and launching our farm over the course of several months—literally getting our hands dirty along the way—would be more likely to resonate with the owners of a brick-and-mortar business than any tale of a digital app company reaching a million dollars in revenue during launch week.

Slowly, we came around to the idea that the fact that we're still here—still alive after all these years—is a story in and of itself. And if we can convince a single reader that starting a small business that serves its community is an endeavor worth pursuing, then this book was worth writing.

Before we started writing a book—before we were Brooklyn Grange—we were just a few individuals trying to find our place and our purpose. But Brooklyn Grange wasn't the product of our existential dilemma, or some guilt over leaving careers many folks would jump at the chance to enter. We were hungry for a sense of agency, sure, but we were not naive. When we met one another and developed the plan to start Brooklyn Grange, we wore no rose-colored glasses. We knew we were taking a huge risk. We knew it would take work to make it work, and that we faced a steep uphill battle. All the while, we watched our friends in the tech world make millions developing virtual farming apps for mobile devices. Yet we chose to pour ourselves into a brick-and-mortar farm that we knew would never see that kind of light-speed return on investment. Hell, we had no idea in those early days whether it was even possible to successfully operate a farm on a rooftop. But we intended to find out.

1

THE CROSSROADS OF COMPLICITY AND CONVICTION

Why We Left Steady Jobs to Take a Chance on a Dream

A s New York City braced itself for an uncertain future, a young Wisconsin transplant by the name of Ben Flanner was wondering what his own future held. For the past couple of years, since earning his bachelor's degree in engineering and moving to the East Coast, Ben had been working as a business consultant, a vocation that afforded him the kind of lifestyle that drives most folks to this city in the first place: an apartment in the hip Lower East Side, annual jaunts to far-off locales, and enough income left over to hit the cocktail bar downstairs often enough to achieve status as a regular.

The job was also challenging enough to keep him engaged week to week. As part of a team of analysts, Ben studied companies to identify which areas of their business gave them the

greatest bang for their buck. Mostly, he looked for the ineffi-
ciencies of a given operation and figured out how to strike those
loss leaders—sometimes shaving millions of dollars from a
budget in the process—without sacrificing too much of the
brand's identity or integrity. Ben was constantly introduced to
new companies and products and would launch himself into
learning everything possible about the surrounding business issues, consumer trends, and prevailing strategies of a given field.

One day, a little over a year into his time at the firm, Ben
was assigned to a team working on a major wine brand. He and
a few colleagues flew to Australia, toured over thousands of
acres of vineyards by plane, and then hunkered down in a
makeshift office stationed in one of the field-side nursery buildings to crack open the books and figure out how to improve
margins. Hour after hour, sixteen-hour day after day, Ben sat
there plugging data into Excel spreadsheets. Each afternoon, as
the sun reached its highest point in the sky, the viticulturists
would head in from the vines to take their lunch. The nursery,
silent save for the quiet clicking of keys, would suddenly crackle
with life as the farmers tracked in clumps of muddy clay, smell-
ing of sweat and grape must, laughing and shouting over stolen
bites of one another's food. As Ben looked on, wistfully, he
found himself yearning for the kind of camaraderie he witnessed among them. He couldn't quite put his finger on what
drew him to envy those Aussie field hands, but envy them he
did, and a sense of restlessness began to nag at him.

Ben knew his job wasn't making him happy: the sixteen-hour days were exhausting, and the pressure was immense. Yet he also knew how fortunate he was to have the opportunities he did. Living in New York City, it's hard to ignore privilege. There are millions of people struggling to get by, and when you're all packed into the same subway car, the haves can't ignore the have-nots. Ben was grateful to have a job where he was learning a valuable and marketable skill, and being the humble guy he is, he felt he had a lot more learning to do. He was also loath to walk away from the progress he'd made toward a successful career. He wasn't happy, but neither was he ready to make a huge career change. So a few weeks after the trip to Australia, when Ben was offered a job in the marketing department at a digital financial-management firm, he took it. The new office was great, and at first seemed to address what he suspected had made him unhappy at his last position: the hours weren't quite as punishing, there was more of a team atmosphere, and the work was less solitary. But as the economy faltered, a sense of agitation permeated the office. No one seemed to be enjoying their jobs any longer, but everyone was acutely aware that they were lucky to have one.

Ben, whom we lovingly refer to as a pathological optimist, tried to make the best of a bad situation. One Friday a month, he would load up a mail cart with all the ingredients he needed to make his colleagues desk-side guacamole and roll it around the office. Other Fridays, he'd don a bow tie and roll through

offering custom root-beer-float service. He invited his coworkers to his cubicle for daily coffee breaks, brewing cups in his
French press and secretly composting the grinds in his desk
drawer after his request to launch an office-wide composting
project was rejected. (Incidentally, he forgot to clean out his illicit compost drawer when he left that job, and it wasn't discovered until months later, when his replacement was hired.)

One day Ben's boss called him into her office.

"You might consider wearing headphones to work tomorrow," she cautioned. "You're going to be fine, but a lot of people
are about to be laid off, and you might not want to hear some of
the things that are going to be said."

Going to work became a lot less fun after that.

Fifteen percent of his colleagues disappeared from their
desks in the weeks that followed. Those who remained began
trying to outshine one another. Changing jobs hadn't made a
difference. Ben's days were still structured around data rather
than people, and he still only used one part of his body—his
brain—to do his work. His hands would often grow cold on the
keyboard as he typed away in the air-conditioned office, and the
sensation made him mildly queasy, as though his body was a
lifeless instrument. Ben found himself counting the minutes till
the end of the day, when he would crowd into a rush-hour train
back home to work on his hobbies: making hot sauce and bit-
ters, and curing meats in his kitchen.

But the hobbies were just that, and Ben was tired of working for the life he wanted to live; he wanted to feel like he was doing his life's work. He had seen people who were happy at their jobs at that Australian vineyard, and he realized he wouldn't be until he was doing something that integrated his body and his mind, something that truly engaged him with the world around him, not just the three walls of a cubicle. More and more often, his thoughts turned to those vineyard workers. He began making weekly trips to the farmer's market in Union Square, and each week the trips grew longer. The more he hung around the farmer's market, asking vendors for tips on pickling this or that vegetable, the more he found himself drawn to their world. He loved the physicality of farming, but more so, he recognized its potential to engage all aspects of his intellect, from selecting the best crops based on flavor and hardiness to engineering more efficient systems to grow them. Perhaps more than any other aspect, he was drawn to the idea of a vocation that was performed as part of a community: by people, for people.

In the summer of 2008, Ben made his decision: the following spring, he would quit, and one way or another, he would become a farmer. So when his job flew him out to a marketing conference in Santa Barbara, he played hooky from the endless string of PowerPoint presentations and ducked out to visit nearby farms. When he got back home, he called in sick to spend the day touring farms in the area. He applied to the agroecology program at University of California at Santa Cruz, and when he wasn't accepted, he didn't miss a beat. He began order-ing farming books online and reading them from cover to cover on the subway commute to and from his midtown office, scrib-bling notes in the margins and dog-earing sections he wanted to reread later on.

One day he was leafing through a copy of *New York Maga-zine*, and a photo jumped out at him. At first, he mistook it for a field of wildflowers, but on second glance, he saw that this pastoral scene was surrounded by a skyline of brick chim-neys and wooden water towers. That's when he realized he was looking not at a rural backyard or city park but at a rooftop. The photo was part of a feature on Chris and Lisa Goode, a couple who had launched a green roofing company after build-ing and falling in love with their own roof garden, on which they raised chickens and bees. Ben was alive with excitement. The simplicity of combining an existing model—green roofs—with the intensive farming methods he had been studying in his spare time struck him as an opportunity to create farmland right here in New York City and, along with it, an opportunity for him to farm!

Beyond being ambitious and having a passion for food and farming, Ben is a systems guy. His background in engineering trained him to look at how things work, the ways in which they don't, and to figure out how to get them to operate more effi-ciently. With rooftop farming, he saw two systems that served each other well. Farming, for example, faces the constant challenge of distribution: no matter how little fossil fuel is used on the farm, the vegetables it produces have to get to the consumer somehow, and that somehow is, for the foreseeable future, going to involve some amount of fossil fuels. On the other hand, urbanites face a lack of green space, yet cash-strapped municipal governments are hard-pressed to build, let alone maintain, them for public use. Urban agriculture addresses these problems— and several others—in a neatly symbiotic way, reducing the amount of energy needed to transport food to consumers and providing usable green spaces for city dwellers to enjoy. Ben didn't waste a moment; he called the Goodes that day.

The amazing thing about New York is that in a city of eight million, sometimes you get lucky and meet the exact person you need to meet in the exact moment you need to meet them. Chris Goode was that person, for that moment. When Ben explained his vision to Chris—that he wanted to transform a rooftop into a productive vegetable farm—Chris could have laughed it off as a pipe dream. Instead, he heard him out and, to Ben's surprise, said, "Yes, I've been thinking the same thing. You start putting together the farming plan, and we'll be in touch. I think I have a location."

The other thing about New York City is that people here seem to be busier than anywhere else in the world, and for a few weeks Ben didn't hear back despite his persistent emails to the Goodes. But instead of abandoning the plan, he only grew more resolved. As winter set in, and Ben's spring quit date approached, he started slipping on work. He was obsessed with the farm. All the bartenders at the watering hole downstairs from his apartment knew about it, and it was all he would talk about with his friends. He hung around the greenmarket chatting up the vendors and asking about whatever aspect of their craft he was most interested in that week. One vendor introduced him to her friend, another grower by the name of Annie Novak. Ben asked her all his usual questions: What farms should he visit? What books should he read? When she asked why he was so interested, and he explained his ambitious plan, she said without hesitation, "I'm in."

All the pieces were in place, except, of course, for the site. Then one day in March, with Ben's quit date rapidly approaching, Chris Goode's name popped up in his inbox. He was writing to say that the location looked like a go, and that it potentially came with installation funds. Ben could hardly believe it. This farm was going to be a reality.

Chris introduced Ben to Tony Argento, a larger-than-life personality in the outer-borough real estate scene, who owned Broadway Stages, a business that hosted film and television shoots. He had made a name for himself building out spaces in areas that were far enough outside the hot neighborhoods to be affordable; in other words, he was savvy. Savvy enough, as it turned out, to identify an opportunity to do something ground-breaking with the roof of his six-thousand-square-foot warehouse in Greenpoint, at the northern edge of Brooklyn. This was a man who wasn't afraid to take a risk and invest the installation costs in the project. This was a man with a long view. (Later, that long view would pay off for Argento when he began hosting fashion and film shoots on the farm. Little did Ben realize it at the time, but this was our first lesson in the "value-added pitch": not everyone will buy into your idea for the same reasons you do. In fact, it hardly mattered whether Argento and the Goodes believed in Ben's vision of creating a road map for urban agriculture entrepreneurs. Argento loved the idea of occasionally using the farm as a set, and the Goodes were happy to score an install job and earn the clout of having built the largest green roof farm in the world.)

The other great thing about New Yorkers is that they're not easily intimidated. Chris and Lisa Goode had previously worked in the film business, so between them and Tony, Ben had found key partners who were used to working with the cranes and construction equipment necessary to build sets and capture sweeping panoramic shots from above. They took the lead on the install, leaving Ben to focus on what he knew and loved best: buying tools, planning the design, and selecting seeds. "I'm going to get the farm up there," Chris said to Ben, "and then it's all you."

So with spring approaching quickly and the last snows thawing on the streets below, Ben watched the dream he'd had for so long come to fruition. The team named the farm Eagle Street, after the address on which it sat, and in that first season,

Ben and Annie labored over shoveling the piles of soil into neat rows later bloomed with kale and cabbages and were dotted with pepper and tomato plants. Before long, the neighborhood caught on and streamed into the raw warehouse space at the top floor to buy their Swiss chard and salad greens. On days the farm stand wasn't open, Ben would load up his cargo tricycle and ride from restaurant to restaurant, hawking fresh herbs and crisp radishes to chefs who were, in equal measure, bemused by the provenance yet impressed by the quality of the just-picked produce. The farm was productive, and Ben was selling out of the crops they grew.

Word of the farm spread rapidly. Press inquiries poured in, from local blogs and newspapers to international TV stations. Everyone seemed to want to know more about the farm tucked away on the roof. One sunny summer afternoon, Lisa Goode called Ben to tell him that the *New York Magazine* reporter who'd authored the piece on her and her family's rooftop garden wanted to write about Eagle Street. The piece was short but accompanied by a full-color photo of the farm, with Ben and Annie squatting in the walkways. It hit stands on the summer solstice, June 21, 2009.

Meanwhile, directly across the river from Eagle Street, in a tenth-floor office in the Flatiron District, I sat in front of my computer, watching the light fade over the Manhattan skyline on the longest day of the year. I was still at my desk in my well-appointed, cheerfully yellow corner office, where I worked as an executive assistant. My boss, restaurateur and winemaker Joe Bastianich, was at the Aspen Food and Wine festival in Colorado, where it was a few hours earlier, which meant I was on call. And the call came: Bastianich had recently discovered a passion for playing rock and roll, and had convinced a few of his celebrity chef cronies to perform some songs at the event. It was one of his first and most public performances, and he was excited. *New York Magazine* was going to blog about it, and he wanted to know the second it ran online. I tried to explain Google Alerts to him; he countered by explaining the refresh button on my browser. I was going to be stuck there all night.

As I sat there trolling the Web site, I was distracted by a photo accompanying a link to another article at the bottom of the page. I clicked, and a field of tidy plants with two figures perched among them appeared on my screen. I read the short paragraph next to the photo describing Eagle Street Rooftop Farm. Then I read it again. I was dumbstruck.

It wasn't my first glimpse of urban agriculture. On the contrary, I'd been thrown into it headlong for the last few months, and like Ben, I had become obsessed. It all started when my friends, a couple of guys who tended bar at my local dive, had told me they were starting a pizzeria on a desolate stretch of Bushwick, Brooklyn. To be honest, I hadn't taken them seriously at first. It seemed like another entry in an oversaturated pizza market, and not a very well-located one at that. But when my friend Patrick Martins, a heavy hitter in the culinary world (who had founded the U.S. chapter of Slow Food and sold meat to my boss's restaurants through a company he'd started called Heritage Foods), mentioned that he was starting a food talk radio station in some shipping containers in the backyard, I figured I'd better see the place for myself.

Suffice it to say, the first time I went to Roberta's in the winter of 2008, I had no idea what I was walking into. The place was all poured concrete and scrap wood. There was no gas line installed, so they heated the freezing cold, mostly empty, cavernous room with space heaters, and boiled pasta water in the pizza oven. The restaurant was decorated with a mix of vintage posters that looked like they'd been stripped off someone's grandparents' ski-lodge walls and hand-drawn cartoons of animals issuing speech bubbles with expletives. Diners would occasionally go without service for twenty minutes at a stretch while the entire waitstaff stepped out in the backyard to shotgun a beer together. It was madness. It was totally punk rock. It was unlike any other restaurant in the world. And if there was one thing I knew, it was the world of restaurants.

Before landing in Bastianich's office, I had worked at one of his eateries, which happened to be among the most successful high-end pizzerias in town. He owned a dozen such restaurants, and a couple of wineries to boot. He was famous, his restaurants were Michelin-starred, and I scarfed down free twenty-course tasting menus like most people gobbled a sandwich from their local deli. On my days off, I blogged about my trips to the market, my meals out, the food I cooked at home . . . but I was hungry for something more.

I had been toying with the idea of leaving my cushy job to get back into magazine writing, which is how I had supported myself through college. I wanted to pen articles for *Gourmet* and *The New Yorker* about our broken food system. Growing up in New York City, I'd always eaten well. My mom would take my sister and me grocery shopping, but instead of filling up a cart at a massive one-stop supermarket, we'd buy our meat at the butcher shop, our bread at the bakery, and our produce at the greenmarket in Union Square. When I went away to college at Vassar, it hit me just how naive my love of food had been and how privileged a perspective I'd had.

I had walked into the dining hall as a freshman expecting to see a bounty of late-summer produce from all the greenmarket vendors who farmed up and down the fertile Hudson Valley. Instead, I found tasteless iceberg lettuce and mealy tomatoes shipped in from hundreds, even thousands, of miles away as part of big corporate contracts. Beyond being downright disgusting, the food left me feeling bloated and sick. From that moment forward, I knew where my passion lay.

I started shadowing two of the owners of Roberta's, Chris Parachini and Brandon Hoy, and Patrick Martins from Heritage Foods all winter with a digital recorder, attempting to craft a story I could pitch to a few editors about the new Brooklyn food scene. It wasn't long before I was distracted by talk of a farming project. They were plotting to plop down gardens atop the shipping containers in the backyard where Patrick's nascent radio station would be housed, as well as in a nearby backyard site some regular diners had offered up. I had a million questions: Where are you going to get the soil? How are you going to get it up there? What are you going to grow? They had none of the answers, but they weren't intimidated. They were just going to do it.

In my twenty-five years on this planet, I had always been taught to plan. I had contingency plans for contingency plans! *Observe, analyze, and comment*—the skill set of the liberal arts–educated college grad. The extent of my capacity to create something was hitting Print on the itinerary for my boss's latest trip. But these guys were, as they used to say, just going to "monster it." It was a term we threw around a lot in the months that followed. "We only have three people showing up today and the soil delivery is late and we have to get two tons of dirt off this sidewalk and through this tenement building into the backyard in five-gallon buckets before it gets dark!"

"Well, I guess we're just going to have to monster it."

You don't come across people like Chris Parachini too often. A former field employee for a private military contractor, he'd spent time in Sierra Leone as a medic, and he isn't afraid of a goddamn thing. Sometimes you wonder if he did half the things he did in life just because someone told him he couldn't. When I was still writing the article—before I abandoned the digital recorder and took up a shovel and bucket myself—Chris wasn't interested in giving me an interview. Maybe it came from his time in a battle zone, but he believed that too much talking and planning deterred from taking action. Actions were the only things in this world that had meaning, and if you didn't like the world you were in, you built yourself a new one.

And he had. In the years that followed, the Roberta's compound was transformed from that cold cement room to a haven buzzing with the low rumble of conversations between neighborhood artists and adventure seekers alighting from the L train. The junkyard next door became a thriving green space, a neighboring building grew to house a commissary kitchen and tasting room, and the ramshackle raised beds we went on to erect in the summer of 2009 grew into two towering hoop houses above the ON AIR sign that glowed red from the broadcasting hub of Heritage Radio. Not much of it was planned; most of it happened organically, as the opportunities arose. But it was a chaos that made sense. In those days, Roberta's seemed in equal measures like the first place to which you'd want to run in the event of an apocalyptic war and the site from which the first rocket would be launched in revolt.

They had opened it on a shoestring budget. According to Chris, they would make weekly trips to the hardware store for screws because they could never afford to buy more than one box at a time. It was a savvy businessperson's nightmare. The neighborhood was full of artists and the working class, not exactly the demographics who spend a lot of their income going out to eat. The location was so off the beaten path that the boys couldn't even get the gas company to schedule an appointment to install a gas line till they'd been open for over a year. But they hadn't let any of this scare them. They believed the neighborhood wanted a place of its own to hang out, to feel at home, a restaurant on its own terms. And so, against the advice of some experts—my boss among them—they monstered that restaurant into being.

Some might call the end result DIY. Others would say it had an "authenticity" that the million-dollar restaurants opening across the river all lacked. At any rate, it was inspiring. Until I began spending all my free time there, I had always imagined myself on a traditional career trajectory: getting a job as an assistant editor at a magazine, helping to research some articles, finally penning one myself, ultimately making editor in chief . . . maybe even writing a book! It had never occurred to me that I could step off the queue and just start something. But that was exactly what the founders of Roberta's had done, and seeing it come to fruition made me giddy. So giddy that I decided to chuck my prestigious CV-building job—a job I'd worked hard to get, a job my parents could brag about—and do something stupid, like give my boss notice in the middle of the worst recession the world had seen in half a century to fight with giant rats over some kale plants.

Back across the river in Manhattan, another Vassar graduate named Gwen Schantz had also made a dumb career move. As a writer and researcher for a nonprofit that lobbied on behalf of water, food, and energy issues, Gwen's job wasn't just one that her parents could brag about, but one she could be proud of while pulling a decent salary and great health insurance. But after a few years of researching, writing, and generally learning too much about the dwindling resources and broken food system failing the global population, Gwen grew frustrated. Her boyfriend of five years and now husband, Christopher St. John, was working at ABC News and felt the same way. Not a night went by when they wouldn't sit at their dinner table and talk about getting out from behind their desks. They needed a change, and it dawned on them that, while they'd traveled most of the globe, they'd really never seen their own country. Maybe Brooklyn wasn't their ultimate destination, they thought. Maybe they could achieve the change they sought more effectively elsewhere. It was time to strike out and see what the rest of the country was doing.

Gwen gave notice in February 2008, after two years at her job, and she and Christopher cleared out their savings accounts.

They bought a standard black Volvo sedan and hit the road. Zigzagging the country, they first cruised south down the East Coast, then cut west, doubling back and wending their way to Washington, D.C., finally heading across the northern United States and into Canada. In June, the two landed in Homer, Alaska, where Gwen found work as a short-order cook in a hippie café making avocado sandwiches to a sound track of the Grateful Dead, while Christopher spent his days working on halibut charter boats and framing houses.

Eventually, the endless daylight waned, and darkness returned to their northern latitude. They had been gone nine months and had made more memories than most people do in a lifetime. But faced with the reality of having to move somewhere and get jobs again, they realized that of all the places they'd seen, they loved Brooklyn the most. So with only the cash in their wallets remaining, and close to ten thousand new miles on their Volvo, they headed back east.

It was now the fall of 2008, and as they drove across the nation's freeways, one thing became clear: getting a job wasn't going to be easy once they got back home. Their long absence had made them realize just how keenly they missed Brooklyn, yet the life they'd left behind was hardly the one to which they found themselves returning. They no longer left their apartment every morning and commuted to cushy Manhattan offices; now they were unemployed and scraping together an income from odd jobs. Gwen parlayed her avocado sandwich–

making skills into a gig working for a friend's catering company. One day her friend mentioned needing help at the pizzeria he managed and offered to teach her the delicate art of flipping pies. And so it was that Gwen went, in the space of one short year, from making a fifty-thousand-dollar annual salary with full benefits to a minimum-wage gig sweating it out in front of a hot oven.

Rather than regretting her choice, Gwen found herself feeling happier and more satisfied. Turns out, being on her feet and working with her hands was a much better fit for her than sitting at a desk all day. But humbler occupations made for a smaller budget, so when Gwen and Christopher returned to Bushwick in 2009, they searched for a place with a backyard where they could grow some of their own food. A backyard in New York City, especially in the types of apartments they could afford, rarely means anything more than a small patch of dirt surrounded by a chain-link fence. The one that came with the apartment they leased had the unique feature of being covered in AstroTurf, which was a blessing because, as they discovered when they pulled it up, it had choked out any weeds! But as they dug into it, they found it embedded with bathroom tiles, animal bones, and the eerie vestige of some previous resident—a dog's choke collar still attached to a thick chain. They spent days clearing the yard of debris and sent a soil sample off to a lab to be tested; it was full of lead. They would need to bring in some fresh dirt.

One day, as I was leaving a garden-planning meeting at Roberta's, I ran into Christopher, who was grabbing a pizza. I had known him and Gwen at Vassar—not well, but enough that I stopped to say hello. We got to chatting and I told him of our plans to build a garden. When I mentioned I was on the hunt for soil, Christopher's eyes lit up. He had tracked down some great dirt from a facility on Long Island, but only needed a fraction of the minimum order they'd deliver. We agreed to follow up via email. When he did, he looped Gwen in as well. And when she came by Roberta's to check it out, her reaction was the same mixture of amused bafflement and cautious admiration I think we all had upon walking into the place for the first time.

She also saw a job opportunity. She was sick of riding her bike halfway across Brooklyn to work her pizza-making job and figured she might as well sling pies in her own neighborhood. Chris and Brandon took a shine to her, too. It didn't take long for them to realize they had a real asset on their hands, a fellow doer, and someone with actual growing experience to boot. When we built the gardens, none of us had given much thought to the fact that we didn't know anything about cultivating crops, and our success had been a mixed bag at best. But Gwen had a knack for plants, and not just at getting them to live. Like she did in her home garden, she nixed any low-value crops that would be cheaper to buy from a wholesale distributor and created a planting schedule so the cooks in the kitchen had some idea of what to expect at any given time.

Within six months of her tinkering for a few minutes before and after her shift, and making to-do lists for me and my ragtag team of volunteers to bang out during our weekend gardening sessions, the Roberta's farm was productive enough that Chris and Brandon pulled Gwen out of the pizza kitchen and put her on the payroll as their farmer. It didn't hurt that they had also acquired the six-thousand-square-foot junkyard next door and needed someone to turn it from a fetid squat for stray cats into a fecund sanctuary blooming with food and festivity.

The lot was a mess. Gwen took a deep breath and dove into the massive job of cleaning it up. It took a forty-yard Dumpster to clear out all the trash, car parts, dead rats, dog shit, and even an errant cat skull. Roberta's, still being a young business operating on a shoestring budget at the time, had zero funds for buying planters, let alone tearing up the entire asphalt lot. So when Brandon told Gwen that the old Rheingold beer factory down the street was being converted into an art studio and event space, she didn't waste any time in asking the building manager if she could help him vacate the space by taking some things off his hands. There, Gwen scored free infrastructure for a ground-level farm that, in the years to come, would bear everything from herbs to fruit trees. Her haul was fifteen massive, thick plastic fish totes, three feet tall and wide by four feet long, with convenient feet designed so a forklift could slide in and move them, which was crucial once they had been filled with soil.

The movable planters were especially important because, as Gwen kept reminding everyone, the garden would never produce as much food as the restaurant would need. Its value would be greater if it could function dually as an events space, which meant keeping it attractive, with a flexible layout that could accommodate different configurations. It's a lesson Gwen still carries with her to this day, and one that she urges the restaurant clients for whom we design growing spaces to consider: an urban farm has value beyond the produce it bears. Additionally, by virtue of its location, it has to accommodate a dense urban population. That often means functioning as a gathering space or in ways you don't even imagine when you're building it out. Incidentally, this was a lesson that would later prove invaluable to our own business as well.

But back then we didn't realize we were learning lessons we would rely on half a decade in the future. Gwen and I were just glad to be doing something other than answering emails and writing memos at a desk. We were glad to be *doing*. Even so, we wanted more. We saw the limitations of the Roberta's project— not just spatially but conceptually. Their farm would always exist in the service of the restaurant, and Gwen and I had no interest in pursuing a career in restaurants, no matter how unique or progressive. Gwen was spending her evenings forming a food co-op in her neighborhood that still operates to this day, and with my newfound revelation that I could start a project of my own, I was toying with the idea of launching a service connecting lawyers with farmers who were being sued by Big Ag companies. Like the owners of Roberta's, we wanted to achieve *measurable* progress, not just work as part of a larger machine creeping toward it.

When we saw the article about Ben and Eagle Street in *New York Magazine*, we saw a picture of just that: doers achieving measurable progress. The rooftop farm had measurable positive impacts on the city's ecological health. It could quantify in pounds the amount of fresh produce it made accessible to its local residents, without the use of any fossil fuels whatsoever. It could even calculate the number of people who visited and witnessed their food being grown, or simply enjoyed the green space.

But more than anything, we saw in Ben a kindred spirit, someone who had done as Roberta's had and built something totally unexpected. On a practical level, we were excited to connect with him and compare notes on which crops worked best and which didn't. We were curious about what soil amendments he used to fertilize his farm and where he got his seeds. We also wanted to meet the man who had successfully built a farm on a roof! So I emailed him, and to this day none of us can believe he actually emailed me back, let alone the very same afternoon. (Farmers in summer aren't exactly staring at their inboxes all day.) But he did, and before we knew it, we were trading visits to one another's aerial growing spaces.

Over the following weeks, we met with increasing frequency. In the beginning, these meetings often centered on our current projects. We'd swing by to borrow or return a tool and end up chatting about whether to split a bulk order of seeds. But as the afterglow of building our respective projects began to fade and we all got a look at the big picture, we started to wonder what the next chapter held. Chris and Brandon were running the numbers on what they'd spent installing and maintaining their garden versus how much they'd saved on produce ordering, which led them to ask Ben what his financials looked like. He shared that the farm had grossed—not netted, but grossed—$13,000 during that first season at Eagle Street, and confessed that he would be taking an off-season job as a line cook to make ends meet.

It's hard to say exactly what happened next, what it was that drove us to band together and start a business. Perhaps it had something to do with the radical climate fomenting as the depth of Wall Street's fraud became clear; it galvanized us. None of us wanted to feel complicit in the greed of the financial industry, of course, but it was more than that: we were compelled to prove that there was an alternative. At the very least, we had been stripped of the idealism that goodwill and humanity held more sway in our economy than the power of the dollar. More and more, when we got together to catch up over a coffee that autumn, the conversation turned to numbers. We found ourselves asking not whether urban agriculture could feed cities of the future—we knew it couldn't—but, rather, whether an urban agriculture business, which was inherently committed to environmental stewardship and community engagement, could be fiscally sustainable as well. We never explicitly articulated it to one another, or even to ourselves, but each of us was driven to dispel the notion that business and greed were intrinsically linked. We were determined to prove there was space for compassion in commerce.

It didn't hurt that urban agriculture seemed like an endeavor perfectly suited to each of us and, moreover, that our personalities complemented one another's. Chris loves to launch projects—like a shark, he seems to thrive only when moving forward. Ben needs a challenge, and writing a business plan for a fiscally solvent rooftop farm was certainly challenging. Gwen doesn't like theorizing about things for longer than thirty seconds. Once she's decided an idea is good, she wants to act on it. Brandon can rally support better than a mascot during the final seconds of a championship game—if he's rallying for something he believes in.

We all agreed that our hometown needed more agriculture practiced within its borders, but having practiced it ourselves, we realized there was a reason the existing urban agriculture projects relied on grant funding to sustain themselves. Farming is a humble business, and New York City has little room for humble businesses. Yet we also knew that one only has so much power *advocating* for things. We all shared the belief that running a project profitably was the only way to *prove* possibility. That mutually held conviction was ultimately what propelled those early conversations about our nascent company from passionate lip service about a hypothetical model to the early brainstorms of a business-to-be.

Ben was being approached left and right by candidates who wanted to work with him on a variety of local food projects, but it was our shared goal of creating a business that could grow over time and be replicated in cities all over the world that led him to consider leaving behind the rooftop farm he'd built to work with us. It didn't hurt that he was able to leave it in Annie's good and capable hands, and Eagle Street Rooftop Farm flourishes under her loving direction to this day. But the more time Ben, Gwen, myself, and our friends at Roberta's spent together, the more we realized we had a special kind of chemistry, diverse skills, and shared ambitions. It would take years for us to realize just how special our chemistry was as a team, and even longer to grow that team into what it is today. But back then, in the fall of 2009, it was just beginning to dawn on each of us that we had met the people with whom we wanted to start a business.

2

NEEDLE IN A HAYSTACK

Finding a Home for Our Farm

So there we were, this crew of ambitious, determined folks resolved to take a risk and commit ourselves to an uncertain future. But before we could get down to the brass tacks of building a business, we needed somewhere to put it. And if you think apartment hunting in New York is tough, try convincing a landlord to let a couple of twentysomethings dump a million-plus pounds of soil on top of their building. It's a heck of a lot easier to find sites now that we've been farming successfully for half a decade. In fact, these days, landlords often ask *us* if we're interested in farming their roofs. But back then we were an unknown quantity, and we were looking for a needle in a haystack: among the fifteen thousand acres of rooftops across our five boroughs, we needed to find the perfect site for our farm.

And not just any old roof would do. First, we knew we needed a certain scale. If we were going to spend the time and, more pertinent, the money, on purchasing and installing a green roof system and ten inches of soil, not to mention the fixed costs like salaries and insurance year after year, we would need to make sure we were creating enough revenue to cover those costs. And in a business as variable as farming, it's smart to leave a decent margin of error (or margin of nature, more like it). We needed enough space so that even if ten percent of our crops failed, we would still harvest enough produce to turn a profit.

Luckily for us, Ben had kept excellent records of his yields at Eagle Street over the 2009 season. We used that data to crunch some numbers on just how much revenue a square foot of farming space could yield and, based on that number, how many square feet of rooftop space we would need to lease to be in the black. Eagle Street had grossed $13,000 in revenue from six thousand square feet of growing space. In order to pay off the installation costs (which, in the case of Eagle Street, had been covered by the landlord—a fluke scenario we knew we were unlikely to luck into a second time), as well as a modest living wage for Ben, who would need to be on the roof full-time and therefore unable to take another job, we would need to gross a whole lot more than that. Which meant we would need a lot more space.

We also knew we were unlikely to find another landlord like Tony Argento who would be willing to let us farm his or her roof rent-free, but we had no idea what building owners would expect us to pay. There aren't exactly a whole lot of precedents for commercial real estate deals on rooftops. So instead of seeking out the industry standard, we worked backward from our revenue projections to figure out what we could afford to offer. Interestingly, this is the question we are asked by nascent rooftop farmers more often than any other: "What should I offer to pay in rent?" Of course, making our rent figures public would make it difficult for us to negotiate a better rate with future landlords, so rather than throw out an answer, we advise young farmers to do as we did and figure out what cost their business can bear. In our case, the equation, which would later become the basis for our business plan, took into account certain fixed costs, such as the crane we'd need to lift the soil sacks up to the roof and Ben's salary, and then a whole lot of scaled costs, like the soil and green roof—and, of course, rent, which is typically calculated on a square-foot basis, which would be dependent on the total footprint of the space we were leasing.

It all involved a certain amount of guesswork, but it was the kind of modeling that Ben lived for, and for which his years as an analyst had prepared him well. How much risk we took on was directly proportionate to the potential for reward, and striking the right balance would make or break our nascent business. If we were conservative and leased a smaller building, we would be looking at lower costs when it came to rent, soil, and green roof materials; yet our revenues would always be limited to the yields we could generate on that amount of space. On the other hand, if we took a bit of a leap and leased a larger roof, we would indeed have to spend more on those scaled items, yet we could spread our fixed costs, like the crane and Ben's salary, over a greater area, and generate more revenue each season, with the goal of banking profits and growing our business over time.

When we compared our fixed installation costs plus anticipated ongoing overhead costs to the per-square-foot revenue Ben had estimated, we found we would need at least twenty-five thousand square feet to break even and pay a small amount of rent, though we liked the revenue figures of leasing a forty-thousand-square-foot roof even better. For those of you who have no idea what the heck forty thousand square feet looks like, it's just shy of an acre, or about five-sixths of a football field, minus the end zones. That's a damn big building, and pretty easy to identify when scanning the industrial areas of the city on a Google satellite map, which is exactly what we did.

Size was our paramount concern, sure, but not our only one. We were also looking for strength. Structurally reinforcing a building would cost us more than we would make back on produce revenue, so we had to find a building that was already equipped to handle the weight of our operation. A cubic foot of green roof soil weighs between sixty and eighty-five pounds when fully saturated, which is always how the weight of green roof components should be calculated. Considering the additional weight of snow in winter and people farming, we were looking for a building that could accommodate somewhere in the neighborhood of one hundred pounds per square foot.

Typically, when it comes to buildings, the old adage is true: they don't make 'em like they used to. This is especially true of big buildings, the size of which indicates they were built as manufacturing centers or warehouses. We've found that a prewar construction date is a good indication that underneath the facade, the structure is rock solid. During the first half of the twentieth century, most industrial buildings were erected with a continuous frame from the ground up made of concrete-encased structural steel and densely spaced columns: perfect for our purposes. We'll call this the Three Little Pigs Criterion: stone house good, straw house bad.

Unfortunately for us, we didn't have a big bad wolf to bring to site visits, and it was too expensive to engage a structural engineer for an assessment of every big building we saw on the map. Instead, as we identified buildings large enough to make sense for our model, we did a bit of Internet research in advance to see if we could figure out when the structure was built. Once we'd plugged the address into a Web browser and taken a look at the satellite image to determine that the roof was relatively clear of cooling and heating units and skylights and such, we consulted a map that showed the year of construction and the building's total footprint (in New York City, this info is available on the Web site OasisNYC).

There were a million other criteria we took into consideration when assessing potential sites for our farm. Location was key. We wanted to be near major roadways for ease of distribution but central enough to public transportation and a residential neighborhood to be integrated into the social fabric of the community. Height was another important attribute. While low buildings make for an easier installation process, they're also in danger of being shaded out by taller surrounding structures, and even if there weren't any at the time of our visit, there was always the looming specter of new construction, which in this town tends to pop up like weeds in a wet July. A parking lot or decrepit old warehouse with a big FOR SALE sign on it screamed, "Tear me down and replace me with a luxury high-rise!"—and sent us running for the hills.

All that taken into account, of the fifteen thousand acres of rooftop space across the city, physical attributes alone whittled our options down to a couple dozen ideal sites. We knew that, of those sites, even fewer would meet the additional criteria that made a location desirable for us, most of which weren't determinable from Google Earth. We needed to go on a site visit to really be sure. But more often than not, we either couldn't find contact info for a building manager or simply couldn't get them to call us back. So a site visit usually meant showing up at the loading dock, asking some forklift operator if his landlord was on the premises, and if not, talking the guy into letting us poke around. Gwen is especially good at this: on more than one occasion, she's walked right into a building, found an elevator, showed herself up to the top floor, and blithely ignored the ROOF IS ALARMED sign—and the ensuing deafening siren.

We were looking at a few key aspects on those site visits. First off, the spacing between the structural columns, or beams, that support the vertical height of a building is a great visual clue as to a structure's integrity. Twenty feet or less is promising, though seeing this density at ground level doesn't mean much. Often, buildings will have adequate support on the first floor but practically none on upper levels. So we would make our way to the top floor and check out the column spacing. From there, it was usually pretty clear what the ceiling was made of, but sometimes further poking around was in order. If there was a drop ceiling and the landlord was friendly enough (or no one was around to stop us), we would ask to push back a tile and take a peek with a flashlight, at which point we had visual confirmation of the building materials used. If the roof seemed to be concrete with loads of pillar support and I-beams, we knew we were in good shape.

Then we would head upstairs. Sometimes this literally meant heading up actual stairs—many, many stairs. We've used our cell phones to light our way through dark vestibules, braved ladders being held in place by one rusty bolt, and accidentally roused nests of roosting pigeons, giving ourselves a good scare in the process. Stairs are kind of great for providing another key insight: the building's culture. What are our future downstairs neighbors like, and how will they react to a farm on the roof? If the stairs are brightly lit and you're passing by women in suits who've stepped out of the office to take personal calls in hushed tones, it's probably a pretty professional environment. On the other hand, you might be sidestepping cigarette butts, blunt wrappers, and used prophylactics. Hey, this isn't Mister Rogers' Neighborhood; it's New York City. And while we weren't thrilled with the prospect of sweeping up those items every time we had guests coming to the farm, we could also be pretty confident that Smokey the Casanova was never going to complain about a little dirt in the hallway.

We also rode more freight elevators than we could count during those early site visits. We grew pretty fond of these lifts, since, for starters, their presence meant we wouldn't have to haul buckets of compost and mulch up several flights of steps. Our fondness made us connoisseurs: from the old dinosaurs with pull-down gates that took two of us to heave shut to the Cadillacs of the freight world, with automatic doors and lacquered-wood walls, we saw it all. We even saw one such hoist, bigger than Ben's apartment, with a full-time operator who'd built himself an office inside, outfitted with a coffee maker, a radio, a recliner, and a framed print of Dalí's *The Persistence of Memory*.

But our favorite freight elevators were those that opened up right onto the roof. If there was no rooftop access beyond a ladder or a staircase, we knew we would have a long road of tough negotiations with our future landlord ahead of us. Elevators aren't cheap to build, but they're important to our business. Not only do we need to drag our materials up there, but what grows up must come down. In spring, when we're just harvesting salad greens and herbs, running a stack of lightweight cases down the stairs is doable. But in midsummer, with those same greens wilting every moment they're out of the walk-in cooler, the many trips necessary to lug hundreds of pounds of cucumbers, tomatoes, squash, and eggplants just aren't tenable. And if the building is occupied by professionals in suits, our neighbors might not be too keen on hosting clients for meetings if they have to share a passenger elevator with sweaty farmers.

Elevators weren't the only negotiation we would have to navigate. Occasionally we'd find a promising building with a roof that was ripped to pieces, in which case we'd try to engage the landlord in a conversation about resurfacing it. This is expensive, but most building owners are willing to discuss it because nobody wants a leaky roof, and they're going to have trouble leasing a top-floor space to anyone if it rains indoors every time it's precipitating outside. And New York City, like many older cities that suffer from storm water management issues (see Chapter 5 for more on this) offers a one-time property tax abatement to any building owner who installs a green roof.

We often mentioned this incentive in our initial call or email to landlords in order to entice them to at least entertain a conversation with us. Typically, if we hooked them with the tax break, that meant their primary motivation was money, and their next question was what we were offering in rent. It wasn't much, and we knew it would be a hard sell, but we figured it was found money for them. With a few exceptions, rooftops are more or less unusable, and therefore a little rental income is better than no rental income. Solar power is certainly a great option for farsighted landlords, but isn't mutually exclusive of a farm, since solar panels can be installed alongside a green roof to really maximize energy efficiency. Cell phone and satellite companies are also in the market for rooftop space, but because they take up so little space and require so little maintenance, building owners can't charge all that much to host them. These days, we do see some competition from fellow urban farmers and the residential and commercial tenants to whom landlords are increasingly starting to lease rooftop space as an amenity. But back in the fall of 2009, we were pretty much the only folks asking building owners to rent their entire rooftop. So when we approached landlords in that first search effort, they were often curious but dubious. Most of them entertained an initial meeting, but our low rent offer and the unprecedented nature of our project scared off owner after owner.

As the autumn wore on, the tenor of our search for a site began to change. We had seen dozens of roofs, and none had been right. Either they had insurmountable physical flaws, or the landlords, cautious about our business plan, were offering leases of only a few years or asking for far more money than we had budgeted for rent. We were eager to launch our business the following spring, which meant beginning the installation before the last frost, but we weren't so eager that we would sign a bad deal. We would have been monumentally stupid to accept a two- or three-year lease, which would have given the landlord the latitude to raise the rent on us significantly after the term was up. Unlike a restaurant, which might grow more popular as time passes and begin grossing higher and higher numbers, our business and the revenue it generated were firmly locked into the amount of space we had in which to grow produce. The rent we were offering was a conservative estimate of the rent we could afford, now and in the future. Evidently, that number did not impress potential landlords.

Beggars can't be choosers, as they say, and there were certainly times when our elevator pitch felt like begging. On one particularly rainy day in the fall of 2009, Gwen and Brandon braved downpours looking at several sites, the last of which was a family-owned Thai noodle manufacturer. When the two bedraggled, sopping-wet farmers arrived at the door, the family felt so sorry for them that they invited them to sit down for lunch. A few bowls of steaming-hot *tom yum* soup later, Gwen and Brandon were indeed begging these particular folks to rent us their roof. Unfortunately, it wasn't a good fit, so we kept marching on in search of the right building.

Around that same time, not far from the noodle plant, we

visited a big warehouse. Built like a rock and only one story tall, hauling our materials up from street level would have been a breeze. But when Ben went inside with the landlord, he saw a puddle the size of a small lake in the middle of the floor, obviously caused by leaks in the roof. When he pointed out that the leaks would need to be fixed before we could proceed with installing a farm, the owner assured him it would be no problem. Then, from across the warehouse floor, he heard a loud guffaw. There stood the current tenant, arms folded across his chest, watching the conversation transpire with an amused smirk. He met Ben's eyes and winked. "He's been telling me that for years," he confided. "That roof ain't ever getting patched."

By the time winter rolled around, we were growing anxious. So when we got a call from a broker whose client owned a structurally sound building with a flat roof right in Bushwick, not far from Roberta's, saying that the landlord loved the idea and was willing to entertain our offer, we were ecstatic. The drawback was that his roof was only twenty-five thousand square feet—the bare minimum expanse of space we needed in order to make ends meet. But with our business incorporation filed with the state, money coming in from fund-raisers (more on that in the next chapter), and the farm garnering attention from the press and public alike, we didn't exactly feel like we were in a position to be picky. We started drafting a lease.

Two months later, we were in the home stretch of negotiations on an agreement. After a discouraging initial meeting in the conference room of the real estate broker representing the landlord, wherein they wouldn't budge on their annual rental rate of $1 per square foot, we had made progress. A second meeting had gone better after we realized we needed to show them a business plan detailing our operating budget. Rather than simply claiming we could only afford to pay a certain amount, Ben created a series of financial projection charts and graphs with detailed estimates of yields and revenues. The new and improved business deck outlined a strong plan to generate enough income to pay rent through the entire term of our lease, but more importantly, it showed that a dollar per foot would bankrupt our business. If this guy was serious about having us farm his roof, he would need to accept less money for it.

So when the landlord took the charts home and everybody parted ways with smiles and handshakes, we thought we had a deal. We had made major concessions on some terms but were staying positive and focusing on how excited we were to be moving forward with the project. With spring around the corner and our seed packets arriving by mail, we were under the gun to start planning the install. We were also doing everything we could to get our name out in the community. On our way to a local food event one evening, where we would be manning a table with info about our project and gathering names and emails of interested potential customers, Chris got a call from the broker who had been negotiating the deal. By the time he hung up, he looked irate. The chain of expletives he issued next did not bode well.

"He's sticking to a dollar a foot," Chris told us, his face growing red. We were in the midst of setting up our table, and had just put out a neat stack of hand-cut postcards printed with the rather bombastic claim "Brooklyn Grange Farm: Coming to a Neighborhood Rooftop Near You!" Except we weren't. At a dollar a foot, we were going nowhere, fast.

We had to talk Chris down from sending an email with language that would have made a sailor blush. There was no use trying to argue with the landlord; he'd clearly gotten cold feet, and sticking to his guns at the eleventh hour was his way of extricating himself from the deal. He knew we would walk because he knew we had no other option. So in mid-February, with the last frost looming on the horizon, the contributions of supporters in the bank, and some impressive press clippings, we found ourselves without a space once again.

Once we recovered from the shock, we hit the ground running. Everyone mapped a section of the city and we started scanning Google Earth for buildings with big footprints. It was back to the rickety ladders and leaky warehouses. Our hopes would rise upon finding a seemingly perfect roof, only to be dashed again as a ventilation fan powered on and blasted it with chemical fumes from some workshop below. We looked at the roofs of local beer distributors, Chinese food–menu print houses, party-rental warehouses, dollar-store junk suppliers,

and lumber depots. Nothing fit the bill, and the disappointment, day after day, was crushing. We tried to keep the faith.
We continued to raise funds in tandem with our search, which
was no easy task without the reassurance of a lease, and we
started thousands of seedlings in the greenhouse behind Roberta's on schedule for spring transplanting dates. But our smiles
were forced. Even Ben's midwestern cheer began to wear thin.

What we didn't realize was that we had been barking up the
wrong tree entirely. The buildings we were looking at were
physically fit for a farm, but it was who and what was occupy-
ing the building that would prove the most influential element
in striking a deal. The massive warehouses around the city
were mostly owned by old-timers who had a good thing going
and didn't want to rock the boat. Their manufacturing tenants
didn't pay much, but they also didn't complain about the crum-
bling loading docks or the toilet that always backed up in the
men's room. These guys appreciated the status quo. Sure, a little
extra money in their pockets wouldn't hurt, but no matter how
much assurance we gave them, they were loath to deal with the
headache they anticipated a big project like ours would cause.
Half the time, they were just waiting out the clock hoping that
the neighborhood in which their property was located would be
rezoned from industrial to residential, which would allow them
to sell their building at a huge profit to a developer who would
raze it and build a condo in its stead. There was an entirely different side of real estate we needed to tap into, and though we

had no idea at the time, we were about to gain an introduction to that world.

As the seedlings started to outgrow their cells and the snow on the sidewalk melted to an ashy gray sludge, we all began to quietly question the wisdom of leaving behind jobs with solid paychecks for what now seemed like a pipe dream. Sleep deprived, white knuckled, and with nails bitten, we still met every day in the shipping container behind Roberta's, and that's where we were when Chris got a call from his cousin who worked in real estate.

"You guys aren't still looking for a roof, are ya?"

Within minutes, we were in Chris's Subaru, speeding down the Brooklyn-Queens Expressway, blasting Hot 97 on the radio. I had scrawled the address of the building on a cocktail napkin while Chris repeated it over the phone, and I picked at the corners nervously on the ride over. The sky was a bright blue and it was mercifully warm—the kind of early spring day that mocks you into thinking the worst of winter is over. As we crested the bridge over the railway yard in Long Island City, Queens, and the building came into view, its bright white facade gave off a blinding glare in the midday sun. Stretching the length of two city blocks and towering above the gulley of parked Amtrak cars in the train lot beneath it, the massive structure seemed a city unto itself, a utopia shining on a hill.

The canned air in the lobby brought us back to reality. As usual, we were introduced to a line of men in suits—always men, always suited. There were handshakes, and business cards emerged from pockets and silver cases, passed across outstretched arms with starched cuffs. The building's owners, Jeff Rosenblum and Ashish Dua of Acumen Capital Partners, were young, affable guys. Outwardly, we maintained composure, smiling pleasantly, maintaining eye contact as we glanced sidelong at the columns bisecting the floors every few feet. With the requisite niceties finally exchanged, we made our way up an elevator and a solid concrete flight of stairs that looked like it could withstand blasts from tank weaponry. We heard ourselves pitching the owners, but our minds were elsewhere, already ten inches deep in soil, transplanting leggy seedlings.

The roof wasn't perfect. For starters, while the location was amazing, perfectly situated between two culturally vibrant areas, it was in Queens. Based on the first site, and the fact that we all lived in Brooklyn, we'd already incorporated under the name *Brooklyn* Grange, which we knew wasn't going to curry us favor with our new neighbors. Hindsight is twenty-twenty, and in retrospect, it was a hasty and poor decision on our part to give ourselves a name before we had a site. We had planned on expanding to multiple locations from the outset and should have anticipated the possibility that we would land in a borough besides Brooklyn. The Brooklyn-Queens rivalry is deep and long-standing but seemed more pronounced than ever at the time. As the Brooklyn brand had garnered mounting attention in recent years, many Queens residents became increasingly wary of a business movement they identified as belonging to hipster transplants capitalizing on the trendiness of their adopted home. There was a lot of derisive chatter poking fun at the *artisanal* this and the *handmade, small-batch* that coming from their neighboring borough to the south. And here we were, a couple of twentysomethings in L.L.Bean boots and Stormy Kromer hats talking about the health benefits of fresh, organically grown produce. For no-nonsense, proudly working-class Queens residents, that might have been enough to paint us as precious poseurs. But that we came with the Brooklyn moniker sealed our fate. Socially, we would have a big job ahead of us ingratiating ourselves into our new community.

Misnomer notwithstanding, the building had its flaws. The membrane looked a bit worse for wear, and was interrupted every dozen yards or so with mechanicals—big air-conditioning and heating units or vents from the floors beneath. There was no direct elevator access, and the roof was a bizarre, asymmetric shape. But the landlords had just bought the building, and save for the previous owners, Standard Motor Products, who had retained only two of the six floors, it was mostly empty.

As we would realize later, this was the attribute we should have been seeking all along. Acumen needed to attract tenants. And not the low-density, low-paying manufacturing tenants that occupied so many of the warehouses and industrial sites we'd visited over the last several months. They wanted high-density tenants who are accustomed to paying a greater amount per square foot: tech companies, design firms, etc. Perhaps better than we did at the time, Acumen saw the potential for us to draw these tenants in. A green roof—let alone a rooftop farm, which operated a farm stand in the lobby where folks could pick up fresh veggies on their way home at the end of their day—would be a huge amenity. In fact, Acumen had planned on paying for a green roof themselves, they told us, and so they were willing to entertain our rent offer, considering we would cover the cost of installation. They were prepared to work with us on getting a deal together quickly, which included plans to build an elevator to the roof, and they even threw in a small office space for us to sweeten the pot. We nodded amicably and pinched ourselves secretly. We had finally found ourselves a roof on which to farm. Little did we realize, these guys were probably pinching themselves, too: we were offering a small amount of capital in the form of rent, but the cultural capital we brought to the table was our real value.

Now that we have five years of experience under our belts and a reputation as smart operators, we can be a bit choosier about our spaces. Beyond a willingness to work with us to solve existing infrastructural issues, we've learned to look for landlords who are excited not only by the idea of having an intensive green roof on their building, but who also want to encourage a sense of community. These are the folks to whom we will appeal, as community is something we can offer in spades. We love making friends with our neighbors, and the other tenants in the building can play a huge part in our daily lives. The early years at our flagship farm were tough; the building wasn't very densely occupied at first, and most of the tenants who were there worked for Standard Motor Products, so they'd been there for years and, just like the low-density warehouse owners with whom we'd previously tried to strike a deal, were used to a certain status quo. We definitely felt like the new kids on the block, and it was difficult to tiptoe around everyone while installing a farm. After ten solid hours of hard, manual labor, the last thing anyone wants to do is mop up muddy footprints in the bathroom. But after a rough start, we came into the building one day and found a pallet of bricks sitting in the warehouse with a note for us:

Thought you might be able to use these!

Your neighbor

Another day, it was a few bags of Quikrete concrete mix. A few weeks later, the crew who had been filming the Smurfs movie on a soundstage they had temporarily constructed on the first floor wrapped production. Their parting gift to us included a desk, paper, envelopes, staplers . . . pretty much our entire office. David, who runs facilities for Standard Motor Products, gave us a wheelbarrow and two space heaters. The printing company downstairs offered to make postcards and signage for us in exchange for letting them come up and harvest a few things for lunch once in a while. Little by little, we began to feel more at home.

When COFFEED café opened in the lobby of the building in 2012, we were ecstatic. Food neighbors are our favorite, and COFFEED was no exception: not only do they fuel us with bottomless cups of freshly roasted joe, they also help fund our composting system, which processes hundreds of pounds of their spent grounds each week. And on more than one occasion, the owner, Frank, has surprised us at the end of a long day with a pitcher of ice-cold beer, which they get from a small microbrewery in the neighborhood. We call Frank "The Patron Saint of Rooftop Farmers." He doesn't need to do all that he does for us, but he understands something crucial to successful business: together we stand and prosper. By bolstering our business, he ensures that we have even more activity on the roof, which means even more customers for his café.

The beer is awesome, but more than anything, it's this sense of community and collectivization we seek when looking for a site. We look for schools that will send their students up to learn with us, families who will shop at our farm stand, and likeminded businesses with whom we can partner on green initiatives and fun events. If we build a farm in a neighborhood that's cut off from the rest of the city and folks can't access us, it's going to be tough to build that sense of community, so we look for nearby subway or bus lines. At our heart, we're a local business. We're not a digital company; our community is our customer, and our customers make up our community.

Even though every site is different, certain aspects of the search process are the same. Once we've selected the site and vetted the location, we begin drafting the lease. Every lease will be different, and every document will be the product of a long process of negotiations, including but not limited to a share of the tax abatement money, a rent-free period of time to install the farm, rent deferrals in the off-season, etc. Our main goal for a lease and operating agreement with our landlords is that we get a nice long duration for occupancy—we would never sign a lease shorter than ten years, and even then, we'd look for renewal options—and work out what rent will be during this period. Sometimes we agree to a slight incremental rent increase over time, sometimes we agree to a slightly higher rent that's locked in place for the full tenure of our stay. We've entertained conversations about percentage leases, where the landlord gets a base rent and then a share of our revenue. But we would never agree to a short-term lease with no indication of what our rent will be after that period ends, because—and we cannot stress this enough—there is no sense investing funds and energy into a rooftop farm installation only to have to haul all that soil off the roof a few years later when the landlords decide they want to put a swimming pool on top of their building.

A lease can make or break a brick-and-mortar business. We probably signed ours too quickly in that first year, and there are a million little details specific to the business of rooftop farming that we've learned to insist upon since then. If we'd had the luxury of time on our side, we would have shown that first lease to every ally and advisor in our lives. Once the thing is signed, it's signed; a landlord won't retroactively adjust a lease to include terms more favorable to the tenant.

We live by the philosophy that good enough is great, and done is better than perfect. No lease will be perfect, nor will any roof. Yet in order to raise funds, we need a signed lease. If we were inflexible about certain selection criteria, we would never have built a farm in the first place. So while we believe that a bad deal can break a business, we always keep our minds open and our imaginations active.

Having an active imagination wasn't hard to do when we negotiated our lease with the Brooklyn Navy Yard. We were in love with the space; it had so much of what we needed already that there weren't a lot of sticky wickets to negotiate with the landlords. Direct elevator access? How about a freight into which we could drive a MINI Cooper. Waterproof layer on the roof? Try a brand-new, top-of-the-line membrane that ensured we would never have to dig up patches of soil to access leaks. Of course, the company that installed that waterproof surface agreed to extend its warranty to the farm only if they controlled the installation, choosing the company to apply the green roof and managing the project themselves. We knew it was hard enough to get a rooftop farm built when we, for whom everything was at stake, were installing it ourselves, but with a third party at the helm, we knew we wouldn't be able to control delays in the installation process. And we knew how tough it was to make rent in winter months when you have an abbreviated growing season. So we built a clause into the lease stating that if it wasn't done by a certain date—in time for us to get a full cycle of spring crops, like radishes and snap peas, in the soil— we wouldn't pay rent that whole first year.

There were less favorable terms that we found ourselves having to bend on, like the huge amount of roof—over 3 percent of our total growing area—that the Navy Yard insisted on leaving bare as a "utility area" for them to perform mechanical repairs. We fought them on it tooth and nail, though later we would realize how lucky we were: the space would prove more valuable as an events venue than it ever could be under cultivation.

But as much as we were able to bring our experience with the first lease to bear on our negotiations the second time around, the real reason that the process was so smooth is because Brooklyn Grange and the Brooklyn Navy Yard are a match made in heaven. In the Navy Yard's management (the Brooklyn Navy Yard Development Corporation, or BNYDC for short), we had found landlords who wanted us on the roof for all the right reasons: they weren't as motivated by the rent we'd be contributing as they were interested in our cultural capital. To that end, they didn't require approval on the sublease of small parts of the roof to other organizations whose primary activity was farming, such as college gardening clubs or seed savers, because they wanted to encourage us to share the farm with the community as a learning and teaching space. In doing so, we acted as a bridge connecting the three hundred acres of riverfront property that stood behind twelve-foot fences to its neighbors on the other side of the gate. Which was, perhaps, the most valuable lesson of all: reaching a favorable deal is often less about hard negotiating than it is about bringing the right parties to the table. When everyone is approaching the process with the same goals in mind, it's easier to reach consensus.

Identifying the right people, we would learn, was important not only to finding a site and negotiating a lease but to building every aspect of our business. We were so focused in those early days on selling our idea as one that had a financial upside that it often didn't occur to us to ask if we were selling our idea to the right partner. But this lesson would come to bear on other parts of our start-up process. And we were about to learn just how difficult it is to find the right funders.

3

RETURN ON IDEALS

Creative Capital and the New ROI

Once we signed our lease, things got very real, very fast. We were now fully committed to taking possession of the roof and paying rent on that space. The clock was ticking, and, even though we'd started soliciting funds well before we found our site, it was now time to complete our capital raise. We saw how valuable our cultural capital was to the new owner of a building. Now we needed to figure out how to sell investors and lenders on our business; what was valuable to them?

When we'd approached building owners, we'd had at least two tangible deliverables to offer: rent money and a free green roof that would add value to their building and remain in place even if we failed as an organization. The social dimension was the cherry on top. But the quid pro quo relationship between a business start-up and its potential investors is typically a purely fiscal exchange: investor gives business money for equity; equity increases in value proportionately with the growth of business; as business becomes profitable, investor receives money back in the form of dividends and over time ends up getting more money than invested in the first place.

So all we had to do was convince these backers that a rooftop farm—a totally unprecedented venture that was reliant entirely on natural forces—would deliver a healthy return on their investment. In the midst of the worst recession the world had experienced in almost a century, this would prove to be no easy task.

One of the reasons we felt confident launching the business when we did was that Chris had a friend with money who was prepared to come on board as an investor and underwrite the majority of the initial costs. But in early winter 2010 when he was reviewing his finances from the previous year, he realized he wasn't doing as well as he thought and backed out. It was a huge blow, but we weren't going to let it stop us. Plenty of people start businesses without deep-pocketed connections. We'd just have to find other investors. We planned to take on three backers who would finance 90 percent of our start-up costs, leaving us only 10 percent to raise through nontraditional means, such as presold produce or fund-raising events.

When we first drafted a business plan to shop around to potential investors, Ben had put together a start-up budget so we had an idea of just how much capital we needed to raise. An early projection had us up and running on only $165,000, which later increased to $200,000 when we landed the larger site in Long Island City. The vast majority of that money—around 80 percent of it—would be spent on the installation: soil, a crane to lift that soil atop the building, and green roof materials. Added to that were some other nonrecurring setup costs like incorporation filing fees and insurance, tools, irrigation lines, market tables and scales, and, of course, seeds. We added a small line for operating capital, since vegetables take time to grow and we knew we'd need some cash on hand. But it was a bare-bones budget. We were being as frugal as we could.

Unfortunately, so was the rest of the world.

Chris's friend—surprise, surprise—wasn't the only person who was strapped for cash in early 2010. With the economic climate being what it was, most of the candidates who might have otherwise come on board as angel investors with a venture as unprecedented—and therefore unpredictable—as ours had seen their financial portfolios take a huge hit less than two years earlier. As we searched for investors in tandem with our search for a site, the climate was thick with anxiety. These would-be investors were now more likely to hoard cash in shoe boxes under their beds than to sink $50,000 into a project that was little more than a business plan and a pile of seed packets.

A few investment circles were recommended to us who touted themselves as next-generation, eco-conscious, social-enterprise-supportive mavericks. They invested in "green innovations," they said, and "disruptive technologies"—investments that would change the way commerce and our economy worked. But even they proved to be more cautious and traditional than they purported.

Which is not to say those early meetings weren't valuable. As discouraging as it was that the net worth of the individuals with whom we met seemed inversely correlated to the amount of time they spent reading our executive summary, the rejection forced us to hone our pitch. By the time we came to terms with the fact that we were unlikely to find just three wealthy visionaries to finance our whole project, our budget forecast was tighter than ever and we had a solid projection of our cash flow for the first five years of operating.

If our projections were so solid, you might wonder, why not just take out a big bank loan? Ben did speak with several banks, and while the government had lowered interest rates to initiate more lending as the credit markets froze, the best rate we were quoted—somewhere around 10 percent—was still more than we were comfortable with. And even if we made room for a 10 percent interest rate in our financial projections, there was a good chance we'd go through the work of applying for a bank loan only to be rejected. After all, most banks are wary of lending to start-ups and require more years of operating capital than we had—which amounted to exactly zero. We couldn't risk losing time on a rejected loan application, and even if our application had been successful, the funds would have taken months to come through. We needed money faster than that.

So far we'd crossed a single large angel investor or a big bank loan off the list. But private equity investments and smaller loans were still an option. Even individuals, however, would have the same concerns as institutions or investment circles: they all wanted to know "How much have you raised so far?" and "How much skin do you have in the game?" And unfortunately, after a few months of pitching, our answer remained "Not much."

It was time to pony up. First, we needed to show potential investors we were personally committed to the project. So we each pitched in as much as we could—for some of us, everything we had in savings. It amounted to $35,000 among the five of us. Having our assets tied to the business motivated us to complete the capital raise even more and impressed potential investors who saw that we were taking risks with our own money as well as that of outsiders. It's easy to venture other people's funds, but you'll always make more cautious, thoughtful decisions when your personal finances are depending on success. Still, we knew we needed more than our own equity investments to make the project compelling to outsiders—we needed to demonstrate that others had faith in our ideas as well—so we decided to launch a good old-fashioned grassroots fund-raising campaign.

For starters, we would throw some events. Events are always a smart way for a company to introduce itself to its immediate community. You can meet and court your future customers and at the same time demonstrate to potential investors that those future customers, who shelled out cash to show up, are confident your project will have a direct positive impact on their daily lives. And there's no better way to get folks in a receptive mood than with a party. But just what kind of party? We had such a diverse community. From the fresh-food seekers to urban planners to green thumbs looking for a place to ply their craft, we appealed to a broad spectrum of individuals for totally different reasons.

Fortunately, we had a home base just as eclectic: Roberta's. For our first fund-raiser, we decided to throw an epic dinner party: not too casual, yet not too composed. Once the event was planned, we turned to the problem of promotion. Brooklyn Grange had about fifteen people on its mailing list and Roberta's was still new at the time. Neither of us had the reach necessary to sell out an event; we needed help spreading the word.

We'd always planned for the farm to double as an educational space in which to teach urbanites about food and farming, and we wanted to emphasize that in our event. So we partnered with our friends at the Liberty Science Center in Jersey City, New Jersey, who helped market the fund-raiser to their network of parents, educators, and community organizers.

As usual, we tapped any of our connections who could potentially help. Our friend Patrick Martins, the former president of food advocacy organization Slow Food USA, was kind enough to donate heritage-breed pork from his sustainable meat company, Heritage Foods. Carlo, the chef at Roberta's, and his team roasted the pork in the pizza oven and served it atop pillows of cloudlike polenta, surrounded by earthy fall veggies. My old boss, Joe Bastianich, and Mark Ladner, the chef of his four-star restaurant, Del Posto, agreed to be the guests of honor, and Joe even brought his guitar to play a few ditties with our bluegrass band buddies. And of course the entire community of Roberta's came through to help us set up, sell tickets, sling drinks, and run the show.

All in all, the cost of throwing the event was $1,400, and we priced the tickets at $50 each. At the time, it all seemed like a lot—especially when we were four days away from the event and had only broken even, with twenty-eight tickets sold. Looking back on it now and knowing the average check of a typical meal at Roberta's, or the average price of one of the dinners we host on the farm, we realize what a steal it was. Evidently, so did everyone else, because the day before the event, we sold out. The food was incredible, the atmosphere was warm and convivial, and the crowd was an awesome mix of Manhattan restaurant heavy hitters, urban farmers, ecology nerds, and tatted-up Bushwick punks. But the real difference was the auction.

If you're not already good at asking for favors, starting a business will give you some practice, and fast. We called in as many as we could on the donation front, so our auction lots ended up being as ragtag a lineup of services and items as we were a group. Chris's brother, Rob "Bronco" Bryn—a charismatic singer and leader of the band the Wild Yaks—agreed to emcee the auction, and he would point to random people in the crowd, whipping the room into a frenzy as he shouted, sweating and gesticulating wildly, egging on escalating bids. We made a pretty penny on Chris's beat-up old BMW dirt bike, for which we later realized he'd lost the keys. He and Brandon offered up an excursion in their sailboat; our friend Gabe McMackin, then a sous chef at Roberta's, donated a multicourse dinner for six cooked in the comfort of the winner's home. Joe Bastianich bought that lot for $750, then said he'd double it if we could host twelve people instead. It's a testament to what supportive friends we have that neither Chef Gabe nor the owners of Roberta's, who were footing the bill for ingredients on the restaurant's dime, blinked an eye before saying yes. To us, at the time, fifteen hundred bucks made in a moment seemed like a windfall, and perhaps more excitingly, it was progress. We finally had a positive bank balance to show investors.

Emboldened by our beginner's luck, and blown away by the

generosity and enthusiasm with which we'd been met when we begged for help from the first folks we asked, we didn't blink an eye before launching into planning sessions for fundraiser number two: a Friday the Thirteenth party with minimal overhead, which meant we could invite all our twenty- and thirtysomething friends and neighbors who couldn't necessarily afford the ticket price of a fancy affair. Gwen and Chris talked the artist Jules de Balincourt into hosting us in his big, raw studio space in Bushwick; Brandon shanghaied bands to play and got our friends who made beer at a new (and, at the time, little known) brewery called Sixpoint to cut us a deal on some kegs. Chef Gabe came through once again and offered his kitchen skills for the evening, making the single cheapest food he could come up with: grilled cheese sandwiches and a couple of big stockpots of bean soup. We sold both as a meal for $10, and even threw in a free beer.

We were buddies with our friendly, local motorcycle gang, Deth Killers of Bushwick, and they helpfully offered to take on all the design and decor for the event. And that's how a wholesome farming business ended up hosting a party complete with a black light "peep show" photo booth and a rotating burlesque pole for amateurs to try their hand at some dance moves. We can't say for sure how many people came, but they were all still dancing when we flipped the overhead lights on at 4 a.m. (OK, truth be told, we were dancing, too). We ended up netting $3,400, proving that one should never underestimate the appetite of twentysomethings for melted cheese, cold beer, and live music. The cleanup was gnarly, though, and after an hour or two of mopping puke off bathroom floors so the place would be in shipshape for the quinceañera happening there the next day, we vowed not to throw another shindig as raucous as that one.

But we still needed to reach the food people: the chefs and restaurateurs who wanted to see New York City become a productive agricultural landscape supplying a greater share of its needs; and their customers, well-to-do foodies with an insatiable appetite for perfectly ripe heirloom tomatoes and crisp salad greens. Simply put, we needed to reach the Manhattanites. For that crowd, we enlisted Ben's friend Carlos, who owned a townhouse restaurant in Greenwich Village called bobo. Because he wasn't able to extend a discount on his space for a Thursday, Friday, or Saturday night, we decided to throw that fund-raiser on a Monday in hopes that "industry people"—chefs, restaurant managers, bartenders, etc.—would have the day off and be willing to attend.

Call it hubris, but after the success of our first two fundraisers, we were a bit overconfident about our capacity to throw a successful event, and after sourcing cheese donations from the lovely Anne Saxelby, a fellow Brooklyn-based entrepreneur, and wine from our friend Peter Jamros, who worked for a bigdeal distributor, we were all atwitter about this fancy Manhattan soiree we were set to throw. Unfortunately, the plan didn't work quite as well, and we almost canceled because ticket sales were so low. We just didn't know as many people in Greenwich Village as we did on our home turf.

As usual, we pulled it off by the skin of our teeth, filling out the low attendance by comping tickets for friends, family, and anyone we thought would bid on an auction item. And once again, the auction saved the day. A few dinners brought in big bucks, as usual, but the hottest offerings were those for home cooks, most of which were donated and bought by outer-borough supporters. "Woodside Bob"—who got his nickname because of his outspoken advocacy of his neighborhood, Wood-side, Queens, and is, to this day, a loyal customer—got in a bid-ding war with one of Carlos's regulars over a hand-forged knife donated by local artisan shop Cut Brooklyn. The local pickles, cured meats, and homemade hot sauce all brought in decent bids. We made a little more than a thousand dollars between ticket sales and the auction, and met a few deep-pocketed res-taurant regulars, but it almost felt like we did so in spite of the high-end flourishes, not because of them. We learned our lesson there: stick with what you know.

This would prove to be an important lesson that we car-ried with us into future enterprises as well: know your people, and have faith in your community. It's incredible to look back and realize just what a group effort getting the farm up and running really was. Saxelby Cheese and Sixpoint Brewery are now household names in our fair borough. They have their own delivery vehicles, and their products line the shelves at Whole Foods. But at the time, they were tiny businesses just getting their start, and donations like the ones they offered us likely affected their bottom line. Yet they—and the knife forgers, the chefs, the food writers bidding on auction lots—felt it was their responsibility to help change the way food was produced in their city. They stepped up and did what they could to support other small, responsible producers trying to get off the ground. You don't always see that: a community of businesses being cooperative rather than competitive. But Brooklyn business back in 2009 was a team sport.

After three fund-raising events, we had asked for as many favors as we could, and likely sold as many tickets as our small, local network would buy. As important as it was to leverage our connections in requesting support, there was a limit to just how many times our friends and neighbors were going to put on a clean shirt and trek out to whatever restaurant for hors d'oeuvres and an auction. And, of course, there was a limit to how many people we could ask over and over again to donate their space, their skills, their supplies. We knew we needed to be resourceful—or "nontraditional," as they say—with our funding sources.

So we got creative. At one point we began trying to sell futures to chefs and restaurants: $5,000 bought you $3,000 in pre-paid produce, plus a no- to low-interest $2,000 loan, to be paid back over twelve months. But restaurants were wary of prepaying for produce from a farm that had yet to be built, and the idea never took off.

At one point, we entered some Pepsi Web contest. It was so long ago, none of us remembers the exact details, but the prize was something like $15,000, and we were hungry for it, sure we could drum up enough votes to win. The problem was that just to be in the running, you had to upload your project at a specific time, which ended up being about as easy as calling in to a drive-time radio show to win concert tickets. The traffic to the site was so heavy that we kept hitting a brick wall in spite of spending twenty minutes hitting the refresh button over and over again. We couldn't even enter the contest. Back to the drawing board.

It was April by the time our friend Anthony, the *pizzaiolo* at Roberta's (again, a Roberta's community connection) told us about the crowdfunding platform Kickstarter. We were all vaguely aware of what it was, or at least that it existed. It had been mentioned in this or that news source, and the first campaigns were starting to pop up in our social media feeds. But in spring 2010, Kickstarter was less than a year old, and the whole concept of crowdfunding was pretty new. Five years earlier, the concept of microlending had seemed like the next big thing. Web sites like Kiva asked users to lend small, affordable sums, like $25, to entrepreneurs across the globe. The idea was great, enabling wealthy Westerners to gain a greater sense of agency over their vague desire to help, and giving them a one-click escape from the sense of complicity we all struggled with. But by 2010, nobody was really talking about microlending anymore, and we wondered if crowdfunding would be the same story. After telling so many people we had a space lined up, only for the deal to fall apart when the landlord got greedy, we couldn't afford another embarrassment; a failed campaign was out of the question. So it was with no small measure of trepidation that we submitted our project proposal to Anthony's friend at Kickstarter.

It's hard to imagine, now that words like "crowdfunding" are a common part of our lexicon and famous Hollywood directors employ it to raise millions of dollars for their films (we're looking at you, Spike Lee). But our early social media posts encouraging contributions to our cause read like the About page of Kickstarter's Web site if it were written for someone's technologically illiterate grandma: *"Hi friends, we've launched a Kickstarter campaign! Kickstarter is a way for you to support our project, but if we are even a penny short of our 'goal' of $20,000—"* (Can you believe the onions on us, shooting for $20K off the bat?) *"—we won't make a dime! So please help us spread the word and reach our goal!"*

Crowdfunding is part of a new ethos of entrepreneurialism.

Rather than asking for donations, which imply charitable giving; loans, which imply financial interest earned; or investments, which imply some share of equity, Kickstarter campaigns ask "backers" for "pledges." These very terms call to mind the drives for public radio or television stations, platforms made possible by a "crowd" of supporters. Unlike the risk of investing in a start-up that might prove to be a colossal flop, there's reassurance in numbers: the populace deems a project worthy or unworthy of creation. Based on how successful these platforms have been, it seems the world is ready for a kind of public commerce, art, and business that isn't produced and funded by the industrial complex.

Backers' contributions are incentivized with "rewards" that range from classic "pledge drive" swag, like branded T-shirts and tote bags, to whatever product the funds are being raised to produce. A musician raising money for a studio session might distribute copies of her new album, or an artisanal condiment producer might incentivize support with bottles of small-batch ketchup. Our incentive? Besides the usual totes and tees, and vegetables for donations at higher levels, we promised that, once our hive was installed at the farm, we would name a honeybee after every backer who pledged $10 or more.

Over the course of the next several weeks, we badgered our friends, family, and anyone else whose email address we had to support the drive. And while our close community rallied around us with a verve for which we will forever be grateful, it was the support from afar that took us by surprise. We received pledges from more than four hundred supporters all over the world, many of whom we'd never met. Yet there they were, sharing our video on their social media channels and contributing generously. We received messages from backers who lived too far away to ever take advantage of the environmental benefits or fresh produce that we promised, cheering our efforts and wishing us luck.

In some ways, it was baffling to think about a project that celebrated locality at its very core garnering such far-flung support. As crucial as the funds were, the encouragement was perhaps even more so. On the hardest days, when the search for a viable roof became exhausting, or the most promising investor we had on the line declined to come aboard, or we wondered if maybe the whole idea was folly, it bolstered our confidence immeasurably to receive $50 from someone across the globe. If these supporters were willing to put their money on the line for us, then we had to chin up and push onward. Clearly, this thing was bigger than us, bigger than whatever rooftop we'd eventually cultivate. It was bigger even than our local community.

So that's fund-raising in the increasingly globalized, digital age: capital routed through servers, images passed in pixels, big ideas made small enough to convey on a smartphone screen. The local business doing a tangible good thing for its proximal community and a more theoretical solid for the world at large.

The fact that we succeeded gave others confidence. We still get messages from folks asking for advice on their own campaigns. They must think, "Look at these guys. They raised $20,000 from people ten thousand miles away for a project that's only forty-three-thousand square feet in scope!" It's hard to know what to say to them. Our campaign wasn't flashy; we didn't even have a bare roof to show our backers when we first launched it, let alone a rooftop farm. Our video, the component of a crowdfunding drive commonly thought to be of the greatest importance, was mostly just our talking heads, interspersed with some shots of us puttering around in the garden at Roberta's—serviceable, but not about to be nominated for any Academy Awards.

We often advise others launching their own crowdfunding initiatives to seek out friends and related organizations with large social network followings and ask them to share the campaign. We might suggest they provide backers with frequent updates, to maintain excitement about the project, and encourage them to share it with their personal networks. But the truth is, our success had less to do with the format of our Kickstarter appeal or its media collateral than it did with the project for which we were raising funds. What our supporters were buying into was the concept, not the campaign. They appreciated that someone was not only building a local business but charting a road map for others to do the same. They appreciated that the project took real action to create actual change. After all the think pieces and calls to action they'd likely encountered, they appreciated that it was a physical manifestation of the hope they had for greener cities and more ethical food.

Kickstarter was instrumental in helping us realize that our project distinguished itself in that way. That realization in turn allowed us to emphasize those aspects of the farm that spoke to people most: its physicality and its tangibility. Even if they didn't anticipate ever visiting, it seemed to matter to our supporters that we existed in time and space. We had always referred to the farm as a proof of concept intended to show that the model was scalable and replicable. But rather than engaging in a feasibility study, we were prepared to put our money where our mouth was and actually build that model. People were galvanized by the actualization of the idea. In a world of digital everything, our supporters relished the real.

And we're not the only ones. In the spring of 2015, Indie-GoGo, another crowdfunding site, saw their largest-grossing campaign in their history. The project? A new type of beehive that allows apiarists to harvest honey from their frames at the turn of a knob without disturbing the bees within. Though the product met with mixed reactions from practicing apiarists who feared it would encourage the kind of armchair beekeeping that leads to sick hives and the spread of pests and disease, potentially doing more harm than good to the already struggling bee populations, their derision did little to stanch the influx of funds, and the father-and-son team behind Flow™ Hive wrapped up what was originally a drive for $70,000 with a whopping $12.2 million. Their product, like ours, involved physical infrastructure that bridged the link between their supporters and a production system from which they felt increasingly alienated. It gave people a sense of agency. It filled people with the belief that the way things were done now didn't have to be the way they were done forever, and it offered a concrete, corporeal alternative. While we had assumed the concept part of "proof of concept" was what would excite people most, it turned out it was all about the proof, the physical evidence.

In that sense, Kickstarter was a crash course in mission-driven marketing. We learned fast how to get the word out, but more importantly, which words to put out. By the time our campaign drew to a felicitous close, we had gained some momentum and begun receiving nibbles. From individuals interested in investing to journalists who wanted to cover our opening, people had heard of us! For the first time, we found ourselves on the receiving end of inquiries! And now, when we cold-called potential landlords or backers, the conversations were no longer reduced to answering the same question over and over: "You want to build a *what* on a *what now*?!" The concept of fund-raising as a process of friend-raising has never been more apropos than in our case, and our Kickstarter campaign was as key as the time we spent pitching individuals and investment circles in gaining us introductions to folks who were keen to hear more.

Unfortunately, when it came to investing sums larger than the ten-to-twenty-five-dollar pledges that made up most of our Kickstarter contributions, the fact that we were building a brick-and-mortar business probably hurt more than it helped. The reality is that digital businesses are more likely to earn a faster, higher return on investment (ROI) than physical ones, which explains why much of the focus in investment circles in the past few years has been in the tech sector. There are simply limits to how quickly and to what extent a physical business can expand, especially a business rooted firmly in cities, where land is at a premium. Tech start-ups, by contrast, are limited in scale only to their bandwidth, or their server storage capacity. We knew we couldn't compete with the mobile apps and digital streaming services hitting the market, but even once we gave up on finding a couple of deep-pocketed investors to pony up the majority of the start-up capital, we were still confident that with the right approach, we could sell shares, valued at $5,000 each, one or two at a time. Hell, confident or not, we *needed* to: after all those fund-raisers, our Kickstarter, and all but emptying our personal coffers, we had raised less than half of what we'd need to get the farm up and running.

To that end, we knew we'd need our business plan to be rock solid. You can't ask individuals to chip in thousands of dollars without some reasonable assurance they'll make it back. We had used a friend's template to create our business plan, and each of us applied our own core competence to respective sections. Ben, culturally programmed by his years as an analyst to focus on numbers, geeked out on financial projections. I stayed in my office after hours, pulling market research from reports on consumer behavior in food purchasing and chasing down stats on the environmental benefits of green roofs, and poured my energy into the narrative section, describing the cultural community we felt would interest investors who wanted to see a triple-bottom-line business take shape. Gwen boiled down key points into a succinct executive summary and aggregated everyone's contributions into a clean, professional-looking format. Now we just needed to get it in front of the right people.

At some point, a friend of Ben's mentioned that she knew a financial advisor with loads of money, but that he didn't have email. Ben would have to bring him a hard copy of our plan and drop it off at his apartment on the Upper East Side. So he dutifully rode his bike all the way across the bridge and up Second Avenue, and left the plan in the prospective investor's imposing lobby with a staid doorman, who looked quite unsurprised by the request, as though he were accustomed to items being left for this particular tenant. A day or two went by before Ben heard back, and when he finally received a phone call from the mystery man, his reaction wasn't what we had hoped. He would make a donation in a heartbeat, he told Ben—if, that is, we were formed as a nonprofit, so he could get a tax deduction. But he wasn't going to invest. In his opinion, there was no chance we could operate this thing successfully as a for-profit enterprise.

"Do you know how much work this is going to be?" he asked Ben. "This is insane!"

Ben, whose pitches at that point had grown pretty creative— and who had maybe lost just a bit of patience after his round-trip bike ride across the city to deliver a business plan that was now being ripped apart by a guy whose name we didn't even know—replied, "Well, if we go bankrupt it's a write-off, and then it's the same as a deduction!"

Suffice it to say, the gentleman did not opt to purchase a share.

It was interesting to see what parts of the plan spoke to whom. The Wall Street guys dug into the numbers right away and had a litany of follow-up questions. They wanted more cash flow analysis, more details on crops, something their analytical minds could grab on to. The restaurateurs were most excited by the idea of cobranding their business with a farm where they could host dinner events and get first dibs on produce harvested mere hours before delivery.

And then there was Jerry.

Jerry Caldari is one half of Bromley Caldari, the architecture firm of record for our flagship farm building, and we were already in talks with the landlords but not yet fully funded when we received an email from his right-hand man requesting a meeting to learn more about investing. That sit-down was, according to Ben, one of his worst pitches, though it would end up earning us perhaps more investors than any other.

At this point, we were on maybe our tenth version of the business plan, which included far more detailed financial information than earlier iterations. After the tough inquisitions Ben had been through with the Wall Street set, he was super-focused on making the math seem appealing. So there he was at Roberta's, sitting in the crowded dining room with Chris and these architects, trying to flip through the deck and talk numbers over the music blaring on the speakers. But Jerry didn't care about numbers. He was more interested in the restaurant, the shipping container radio station out back, and are these tables handmade from reclaimed wood? In fact, Ben thought he'd lost him at one point, till Chris jumped in and started talking big picture again. That's when we realized Jerry was into it for the concept. He was the rare case who would rather see some good done in this world than realize a quick ROI. Jerry turned out to be more than just a Manhattan architect—he was a do-gooder at heart, and he was willing to put his money where his heart was.

When he emailed and confirmed that he was on board to invest, we were thrilled but not shocked. When he emailed again to introduce us to another potential investor, we were pleasantly surprised. And then . . . he just kept on emailing. It turned out that Jerry had a bunch of similarly big-hearted and optimistic, successful friends. He got us three separate investors and brought in $25,000 worth of capital, more than 10 percent of our total goal. The man was our own personal crusader. (And that was just the beginning; he's gone to bat for us time and time again as our architect.)

At one point, Ben was asked to speak on a panel at the Green Building, an energy-efficient and low-impact event space in lower Brooklyn that had just opened the year prior. Ben said yes to the request figuring that the event would draw a decent crowd of Brooklynites interested in sustainability and green architecture, just the types we wanted to tap not only as potential investors but as Community Supported Agriculture (CSA) members who sign up for a subscription-based weekly share of vegetables, market shoppers, and so on. It was a funny little event, put together by a local advocacy group for some cause or another. None of us even remembers what the panel was about, though we do remember that one of the other panelists was a grower at a place called Paisley Farm and always wore paisley.

Afterward, Ben started helping the organizers fold up and stack chairs—a farmer can't see work that needs to be done without jumping in and lending a hand. Witnessing this was a guy named Gary, who had been in the audience that night. Gary farmed garlic on some family land in Connecticut, and he did so biodynamically, following the cycles of the moon using a homemade lunar calendar that would later earn him the nickname "Lunar Gary" around the farm. But garlic wasn't his livelihood. Gary and his wife ran a successful communications agency and were savvy New York businesspeople. He approached Ben and said he was impressed with not only his remarks on the panel and the concept of the farm but also his willingness to jump in and help out above and beyond the call of duty—the guy liked the fact that Ben, a speaker, was moving tables and stacking chairs. So, too, was Gary willing to jump in and lend a hand, he said.

Not only did Gary end up loaning us a chunk of money, but he also acted as a mentor throughout the fund-raising process. He would often call Ben and check in, asking questions like "You guys getting along? Any fights? If there are fights, tell me." He was practical ("Who is handling the cash? And can you trust her 100 percent?"), and sometimes even pushed us a little when we needed it most ("Where's the lease? You need a lease!"). In some ways, Gary was a bit of a father figure, and as someone might react to their dad's advice, we would occasionally roll our eyes a bit (we know, we know, we need a lease!), but we listened, because he was asking all the right questions, and we knew we were fortunate to have him behind us, watching out for our interests.

Slowly but surely, Ben's relentlessness and optimism paid off, and the funds came together. One afternoon, he met an investor at a restaurant in downtown Manhattan, where he picked up a check for $5,000. Then he hopped on his bike and rode across the Manhattan Bridge to Lunar Gary's apartment in Dumbo where he took another check for a $10,000 loan—and a tequila shot with Gary. Then it was back on the bike, flying up to Bushwick for a Heritage Radio Network interview in the shipping container behind Roberta's. It was a crazy day where everything was happening at once, a feeling we'd get used to quickly in the weeks that followed. By the time Ben locked up his rusty brown Fuji with duct-taped handlebars and a milk-crate basket outside the restaurant, he was completely wired. Nobody would have guessed from looking at him, with his torn corduroys and puffer coat leaking down, but he had $15,000 of other people's money in his pocket.

We'd love to say the debt-equity ratio we raised was a carefully calculated and entirely intentional proportion, but while we were aware that the appropriate amount of debt would be somewhere in the 10 to 20 percent range, the truth is we didn't have that kind of financial freedom. Rather, we let the chips fall. Some backers felt that the risk-reward ratio was high, and if they would only be making 8 percent on a loan anyhow, they'd just as soon be able to call themselves an owner and take the equity and the risk that came with it. Others expressed unapologetically that they were lending instead of investing be-

Our crew unloads a soil supersack during the installation of our flagship farm in Long Island City, Queens. We were a ragtag team, but we got the job done.
(© Donnelly Marks)

One of our many guardian angels, Matt Calender, shovels out a dirt buggy atop freshly lain green roof layers at the flagship farm.

An aerial view of our Queens rooftop. After weeks of work and a few panic-inducing delays, we finally had a farm.

The bare roof of
our Brooklyn Navy
Yard site before
the installation
of our second farm.
*(Image courtesy of
{group theory})*

Ben Flanner, our head farmer,
president, cofounder, and
in-house optimist, overlooks the
installation of the Navy Yard site.
(Image courtesy of {group theory})

BELOW: Our Navy Yard site set
against the lower Manhattan
skyline.

Chase Emmons, Ben Flanner, and
Gwen Schantz survey the farm.

Chase had the crazy idea to start a commercial apiary in New York City.
Here, he tends to a hive at the Navy Yard farm, one of more than
thirty we keep throughout the five boroughs. *(© Esther Horvath)*

Ben and the Navy Yard team transplant tomato
seedlings from trays into larger pots.

Ben harvests at the Navy Yard farm. At Brooklyn Grange,
even the executives get their hands dirty. (© *Valery Rizzo*)

Navy Yard farm manager Matt Jefferson makes a punch list for the day. The work never ends at our farms, which means prioritizing is critical.

The Empire State Building and a bunch of our rainbow carrots. You don't see these bad boys at your typical supermarket.

With the soil spread deep and evenly, we transplanted the very first seedlings onto our flagship farm. Ben can be seen in the background, surveying the brand-new rooftop field.

A dinner at the flagship farm. Having our farms double as event spaces not only makes us more profitable; it also allows us to share our spaces with our community.

A Fourth of July party at the Navy Yard farm.

Director of events Michele Kaufman buses glassware at a farm event.

Yoga on the roof at the Navy Yard.

Financially speaking, chickens are real dogs. But we love them anyway for the life they bring to the roofs, and as an educational tool for City Growers.

Zadie Faye Sharpe is one of the many young New Yorkers growing up—literally and figuratively—on our rooftop farms. (© *Cara Chard*)

cause they figured we would make it for at least five years, which was our original window of loan repayment, but they had their doubts about our longevity beyond that. They wanted to be first in line to be paid back.

Ultimately, our hard work was rewarded, and not only were we able to build one successful location, but after a few years, we were ready to expand to another. Our business plan had outlined a pretty aggressive growth plan: in order to hit the targeted financial milestones outlined therein, we had projected expanding to seven rooftops in our first five years. Needless to say, we were being overly optimistic, but when we got the opportunity to build the Brooklyn Navy Yard farm in 2011, we were ecstatic! Still, we were reluctant to dilute our equity to the degree that a second round of fund-raising would require. We'd already worked so hard and held on to less equity than we'd have liked. And the price tag on the Navy Yard farm, which spanned sixty-five thousand feet as opposed to the flagship's forty-three thousand, would be significantly higher than that of our Queens location. The fact that the roofing company insisted on selecting one of their preapproved licensed green roof applicators to install the farm in order to extend the warranty on the brand-new roof membrane would bump up the price considerably, too.

Fortunately, before we even began identifying all these rising costs, our contact at the Navy Yard alerted us to the fact that the New York City's Department of Environmental Protection (DEP) had designated a good amount of funding to green infrastructure that aided the city's storm water management efforts. It was a total lightbulb moment. We hadn't really considered grants previously as a source of funding, since they are typically applicable only to nonprofits and charitable organizations and we were structured as a limited liability, for-profit corporation. But this grant was available to for-profit landscape architects, urban planning firms, and building owners—anyone who could help the city mitigate the flow of storm water into its sewage system by absorbing runoff (see Chapter 5 for more on this). Not only did our green roof help mitigate runoff, but it also created jobs and opportunities for community engagement. The city approved our application, and we won the grant.

When we laid out the budget for the Navy Yard farm, we were looking at an excess of $800,000. Though the $600,000 grant covered most of the green roof installation costs, since that infrastructure was directly responsible for mitigating runoff, there were certain costs the grant did not cover, like fixing the freight elevator that went all the way to the roof, building a greenhouse, and craning up shipping containers to use as storage space and walk-in coolers for our harvests.

So we launched a second round of fund-raising—only two years after completing our initial capital raise, we were back in the ring. This time around, however, we had hard numbers instead of just projections, a track record of success, and a menagerie of press clips that made our brand recognizable (and our mothers proud). We still had to dilute our equity but not catastrophically so, since Brooklyn Grange was valued at double what it had been back in 2009–2010 before it was a business at all. The Brooklyn Navy Yard was generous with their contributions, buying into the business and paying for the elevator repair costs to get us a working lift up to the roof. Some first-round investors even brought more cash to the table so their equity wouldn't be diluted, while others chose to loan us funds. This time, it was a matter of weeks, not months, before we raised what we needed to complete the build out of our second rooftop location.

But we had no idea, back in the spring of 2010, what the future held. We wish someone could have shown us a crystal ball and reassured us that our farm would be profitable and expanding two short years later. We knew we had earned the faith of our backers, the investors, lenders, and Kickstarter contributors who made our farm possible, not because they expected a big financial return but because they believed we could manifest the hope we'd raised in them. We'd excited a community of supporters with the evidence that there were still new ideas to be realized, and now we had to realize our idea. If people had bought into our business solely based on financial projections, it would have been less pressure: numbers were things outside of ourselves for which we were striving. We could hit them, or we could fall short. But the concept, the hope, the objective . . . these were things for which we, as individuals operating as a team, were culpable. And now we were on the line to make them real.

If we knew then that we would be thriving five years down the road, it would have made what was to come so much easier to take. Yet we had no prophecy to comfort us. Instead, by the time May 2010 rolled around, we had a whole lot of other people's money, a significantly shortened growing season, and a bare roof that we, ourselves, needed to turn into a farm.

4

JUST MONSTER IT

Building the Farm

In the dim, predawn hours of May 10, 2010, a steady murmur of off-duty yellow cabs and newspaper delivery trucks sped along a stretch of Northern Boulevard in Queens best known for car dealerships and discount meat suppliers. The light cast a cool blue hue on the eerily desolate sidewalks. Then, one by one, figures alit from bicycles and others emerged from the subway steps, clutching thermoses of coffee and rubbing sleep from their eyes. We wore boots and pants made of heavy denim and canvas, with bandannas tucked into one back pocket and work gloves into another. In the chilly spring morning, most of us wore wool hats with brimmed baseball caps underneath to keep the sun from our eyes. An observer would have guessed we were construction workers arriving on a job site, and today they would have been right. Today we were here to construct something un-precedented: the world's first commercial green roof farm.

Two eighteen-wheeler flatbed trucks were parked in front of a hulking white building on the six-lane street, and two more trucks were just minutes away on the expressway. Each truck was loaded with fifteen giant, plastic woven bags—aka supersacks—each of which was filled with about 2,700 pounds of soil. There would be 360 of these sacks arriving over the next few days, and already our plan to back the trucks into the load-ing bay and use a pallet jack to move them directly from the flatbed onto the dock had hit a snag: the supersacks had been side loaded, and the pallets on which they were sitting were only accessible from the sides of the trucks. So there they sat, parked in front of the building, taking up the entire right lane. Chris sat in the driver's seat of a forklift, steering it along the outside of the trucks, which meant blocking the center lane as well. All around him and down the block, we stood in the street, hard hatted and reflective vested, waving our orange flags of warn-ing to the cars speeding toward us, their drivers blinded by the rising sun at our backs.

More than once a driver waited until the last minute to merge into the single lane we left for through traffic, leaving the car behind it little time to do the same upon realizing we were there. We waved our flags higher, harder. We whistled through our fingers. We jumped into the air when cars stopped for a red light, so those behind the front line would see us. We placed the traffic cones farther out in the road, edging into the third lane to make sure the cars would have to slow down while passing us. Meanwhile, Chris made trip after trip, one sack at a time, from the truck to the loading dock, where we would pick each sack up with a pallet jack and relay it into an empty warehouse. We had barely unloaded the first truck when the third and fourth ones arrived. They had nowhere to pull up. Horns blared; flags waved.

It wasn't yet six a.m. on a Monday. Our goal was to finish by sundown on Friday. It's a good thing we weren't holding our breath.

Installing a one-acre rooftop farm is no easy task. There are architects and contractors who install green roofs for a living, but they don't come cheap. As a cash-strapped new business, we didn't have the budget to sub out jobs to designers and contractors. It was a do-it-yourself situation, and we were a do-it-yourself kind of team. We lived by that adage we'd learned hanging around Roberta's: just monster it. If we overthought what we were doing at any point, we might have talked ourselves out of it. We knew it was going to be hard work, and that we'd be moving forward blindly at points. But we did our due diligence, planned as much ahead of time as we could, and resigned ourselves to the fact that there were some things we probably weren't anticipating, which we'd address as they came up.

That's not to say we didn't have a pretty impressive core team: Chris had spent time in the military and was a natural foreman. Gwen was raised renovating her parents' old house, so she knew her way around power tools, and I had spent years as an executive assistant, so I made a tight schedule ahead of time, with call sheets listing everyone's contact info and project role. Most importantly, Ben had actually helped out with the installation of a rooftop farm when Eagle Street was constructed, so he knew what materials to get and how to put them together. Between our skills, and Brandon's uncanny ability to rally the Roberta's community to spend their days off on a mercilessly sunny, windy roof shoveling soil, we were confident we could get the job done. What could go wrong?

Once we got the soil unloaded into the warehouse, we started hauling materials up to the roof. We had hired a crane to lift the supersacks and dirt buggies, but crane operators are paid hourly, and we wanted to get as much done as possible before they arrived at seven a.m. So rather than ratchet strap our green roof materials to pallets for them to lift onto the job site, and then have them wait as we installed the first section of green roof in advance of the soil being craned up, we carried the first round of root barrier rolls and filter fabric and stack upon stack of drainage mats into the freight elevator. The elevator only went up to the fifth floor, though, so from there, we carried the heavy, unwieldy materials up the two flights of stairs. As the day broke and the light turned from sunrise gold to the cool bright white of early morning, we stood on the bare roof, sweating in our flannels, surveying our piles of materials. We were cheap in those days. We should have sprung for the extra half hour and craned the lot up. Instead, our work had yet to begin, and we were already exhausted. It would take years before we learned how important labor was, and how to value it accordingly. Back in those days, the dollar ruled, and we didn't spend a red cent unless we absolutely had to.

Perhaps the toughest part of building the flagship farm was the shape and location. Built in 1919, the original structure is a three-hundred-foot-long trapezoid, which is more than twice as wide at the east end than the west. If that weren't tricky enough, a rectangular one-hundred-foot-by-seventy-foot addition had been tacked onto the west end in 1923, so the resulting form is shaped a bit like the letter Y. The roof was also dotted with HVAC mechanical units every dozen yards or so, as well as a sizable water tower and staircase bulkhead right smack dab in the center.

The long, narrow expanse wouldn't have been as much of a challenge had we had access along the north or south sides. But the south side was a railroad yard, and it would have taken months to come to an access agreement with the rail line, if it could have been done at all. The north side faced onto Northern Boulevard, which, in addition to being a busy thoroughfare, was a hollow street with a subway running underneath it. So we were forced to place the crane at one end of the four-hundred-foot-long structure. From there, we would steer our motorized mud buggies into position with their hydraulic buckets nose to nose, in alternating teams of four, and slit the bags open into the buggy buckets. The buggy drivers would run the soil down makeshift plywood "runways" all the way to the far end of the farm, where teams of shovelers were waiting to spread out the soil. Seems simple enough, right?

Well, the soil was just one piece of the puzzle. The other big component of the install was the green roof itself, which was a multilayer system of root barrier, drainage mats, and filter fabric, each of which had to be lined up just so to function optimally. And even if all the layers had been the same dimensions—which of course they weren't—we still had to cut around the various HVAC units, bulkheads, drains, and odd angles. One type of shears worked well on the filter fabric but not on the root barrier, which needed a sharper scissor. The ridged drainage mats were made of such stiff plastic that it took a utility knife to slice through them, which was a hazardous task with rather poor results. If this weren't enough to manage, we had to execute it in step with the mud buggies, laying down a small section of green roof and then promptly dumping soil on top of it before the wind made a mess of the strata.

Keeping a steady rhythm wasn't easy, but it was absolutely essential. If the green roofing teams moved too quickly, the materials would fly around—and in a rooftop wind, that could mean a drainage mat getting caught in an updraft and sailing over the parapet wall toward the busy street below. But if the soil team outpaced the green roofing teams and had to wait for them to catch up, that meant we were paying for a crane that we weren't utilizing at maximum efficiency, which we couldn't afford to do. To ice the cake, we couldn't run the dirt buggies on the bare roof, for fear of tearing up the membrane and causing cracks that would lead to leaks. So with everything else we had going on, we were moving big sheets of plywood around to build runways on which the buggies could drive to whatever section we wanted them to dump next. The boards were heavy, and we didn't have that many hands on deck, so this often meant squatting down and grabbing a board that was larger than some of our wingspans, and then carrying it—rather than dragging it, again, to protect the integrity of the roof—to whatever position in which it needed to be placed.

Had we been experienced green roof installers, this all might have been easier to manage—at least we would have known to give ourselves more time—but we were an amateur and ragtag crew to say the least. In addition to the core team of Ben, Gwen, myself, Chris, Brandon, and half the staff at the restaurant, we called in our friends, families, roommates, neighbors, exes, and whomever else we could get to come lend a hand: anywhere between fifteen and twenty-four people a day. It was a crazy move. No big construction project should ever be undertaken without several experienced members, and our ratio of experienced leaders to novices was dangerously skewed. But with our basically nonexistent budget, we didn't have many options.

What we did have were some real superstars. There was Matt Calender, then a bartender at Roberta's, who would sleep maybe an hour between his closing shift and our early-morning call times, yet never once complained and was often first to arrive; Marshall Korshak, Ben's soft-spoken artist friend, who wore all black, even on the most blistering-hot days; Les Foster, the fire-eating, tribal-tattooed construction manager at Roberta's, who didn't speak so much as shout in a thick British accent, beginning every sentence with "OY!"; and Montana Masback, who brought his overall-clad dad with him to work as an unstoppable father-son team. There was Gabe Rosner, the gun-toting, motorcycle-riding CFO of Roberta's, who always drove the buggy painted with a shark baring its teeth, onto which some previous driver had scrawled the mysterious phrase "No shirping in the dirt buggy." Laena "The Jam Lady" McCarthy was the only woman brave enough to insist that one of the tough guys give up his buggy and let her take a spin. There was Giuseppe Falco, the restaurateur, who brought a million pizzas for lunch one day; and Katherine Wheelock, who weighed about as much as a cubic foot of soil but could shovel out a buggy dump faster than a whirling dervish. That's just to name a few.

The truth is, the outpouring of hard work was overwhelming, and we'll never be able to sufficiently thank all the people who showed up and sweated it out for us in those early days. We thought we'd tapped all the favors we could at the fund-raising stage of the project, but here we were again, asking our friends and loved ones to pitch in. The work was hard, the sun burned us to a crisp no matter how much SPF 60 we slathered on, and the soil . . . the clouds of soil that rose up around each buggy dump would settle upon us and make its way into every orifice, into our very pores. We would blow it out of our noses at the end of each day, and wash handfuls of it out of our hair. Even when we thought we were clean, we would find black soot in the inner corners of our eyes and deep inside our ears. We would fall asleep with the rhythmic *crunch-swoosh* of a shovel scooping dirt and heaving it onto the green roof echoing in our heads: the soil was in our brains.

And in spite of this, our community showed up for us, day in and day out, their only compensation a hearty lunch eaten way too fast and a couple of ice-cold beers at the end of the day, which we would drink in two or three long pulls before heading home and collapsing into bed well before dark. They were troopers, and they gave us the strength to keep pushing through the hardest days. Little did we know, as we flopped onto our beds after a long, hard week that Friday evening, the hardest days were yet to come.

Two of our best friends and most ardent supporters were Eric and Hilary, Ben's college friends from back in Wisconsin, who shared his good nature and relentless positivity. Unfortunately for us, they both enjoyed full-time jobs that made it impossible for them to join our install team, as we worked on weekdays to avoid paying the crane guys overtime. But they offered to come by on weekends to lend a hand, watering the freshly seeded beds and taking photos to help us document the process. Around nine a.m. on Saturday morning, the sixth day of the install, which was already taking longer than we anticipated, we were all down at the Roberta's greenhouse tending to our seedlings, which were growing more and more root-bound by the hour, when Ben's phone rang. It was Eric on the line, and when he spoke, there was no trace of his usual cheer; Ben knew immediately that he did not have good news.

The previous evening, once we'd all left for the day, the NYC Department of Buildings (or DOB, for short) had issued a Stop Work Order on the job. The big white papers were plastered over the door of the building, halting Eric and Hilary in their tracks. They snapped a photo with their phone and sent it over. The order stated that we were in violation of the law for failing to obtain a permit for work.

We were shell-shocked. We had, of course, a structural engineer's report certifying that the building could withstand the weight of our soil, and an architect's blessing. It wasn't that we'd used any prohibited materials, designs, or methods of installation, but simply that we hadn't filed our plan with the city and received documentation from them, because we'd been told by every industry professional with whom we'd spoken that they didn't file their green roof installations. A green roof, we'd been assured, was not a "major alteration," or new structure, which we had been advised were the designations that would trigger the requirement to file a DOB permit for the project. And we had believed our colleagues without qualification, because, we figured, they were professionals. They knew what they were doing.

Which brings up another important point: just because people have credentials doesn't mean they're infallible. When you are uncertain about your own competence, it's easy to assume everyone around you knows more than you do. Hell, there were moments during the install when I wondered what I was doing there. I wasn't strong or handy like Gwen, nor did I have a brain for systems optimization like Ben. Chris knew all the jargon the crane guys used, and he and Brandon had a restaurant build-out under their belts. I figured they all must have thought I was total deadweight. It took me years to be confident in my own value, and only upon reflecting on those early days with all the wisdom that hindsight brings did I realize that I wasn't the only one who felt that way. We all have moments of feeling completely out of our depth. Ben and Gwen were totally flying by the seat of their pants during the install process, too. We were counting on Chris and Brandon's construction experience building the restaurant and the advice of our colleagues in the field. And, as it turns out, even *they* weren't totally clear on the rules!

That's the trick to overcoming insecurity when taking on something new. Sure, you're going to feel like a fraud sometimes, but instead of fretting over whether, at any moment, everyone is going to figure out you have no clue what you're doing, reassure yourself that they're all too busy worrying about the same thing to notice you. And when you do screw up, don't let it shake your confidence. Just because you flubbed one thing doesn't mean you're incompetent. Sometimes, when monstering, you fall flat on your face. They say to fake it till you make it; we say monster it till you learn how to do it right.

And rest assured, most everyone else is doing the same thing. It was the very self-assurance of those industry professionals that had made us believe them. We were so green, we figured, and they were so seasoned that any doubts we might have had were outweighed by our confidence in them. Plus, we'd been relieved to receive the advice to move forward without permits, because a job the size and scale of ours was guaranteed to take time and money to approve, since nothing like it had ever been built before.

Taking the advice of those folks to proceed without permits wasn't pure naïveté on our part. If we'd wanted to be totally certain, we could have hired an expediter who knew city laws inside and out. That, of course, would have cost us money that we didn't have. We could have made some calls and tried to get confirmation from the powers-that-be that we were in the clear, but facing down the ticking time bomb of the season, we simply weren't as diligent as we would have liked. The truth is, in some situations, it's necessary to operate under the premise that it's better to ask for forgiveness than permission. That was the gist of our colleagues' advice to us: there may, technically, be some permits we *could* file, but we didn't need to file them, and no one would ever know or care. That may sound like really bad advice, but we've found that occasionally, there are old, draconian rules in place from long-forgotten times that are no longer relevant, and those tasked with enforcing them would rather not be bothered at all. This, unfortunately, was not one of those situations. The trick is to know which rules those are, ask questions, and take calculated risks rather than blind ones.

Sometimes, however, you don't have the luxury of making the choice at all. For us, it was a very real possibility that, given our time line, if we had asked the authorities to green light our project, we would never have gotten up and running in time to make ends meet that first season. We might have been told to hold off until they were able to send an assessor themselves, which would have set us back catastrophically. We might have found ourselves at the bottom of a long list of projects pending approval. Or we might have lucked out and reached someone who believed in green infrastructure and held our hands through the process. We'll never know, because we decided to just monster it.

As it turns out, a building permit is necessary anytime you're doing work of any sort. The big difference between us and our colleagues was that they did their work quietly and invisibly, above sight lines of the public and of regulating officials. We, on the other hand, were issuing press releases. It was wishful thinking on our part to believe that the media we'd allowed up to cover the install—from the *Daily News* to the *New York Times*—wouldn't have raised red flags with the authorities. That was the real boneheaded move: you can't have your cake and eat it, too. You can have the visibility, or you can skate under the radar. But when you crow about something that's happening so publicly, the city can't turn a blind eye. We were asking for it, big-time.

Perhaps for that reason—and just to make matters worse—the DOB had extended the order to cover all work in the entire building—presumably to make sure our landlords took it seriously, too. Which, given the fact that they had about fifteen different projects under way on various floors as they worked to convert the building from a single-tenant space to a multitenant commercial development, they did. Great foot to get off on with your new landlord, huh?

And if that weren't all bad enough, we got slapped with the order on a Friday afternoon, so we were spinning our wheels all weekend waiting for the city to arrive back at their desks on Monday morning. But when they did, we were ready. After a lot of off-hours phone calls and meetings between with new landlords, and the help of an old friend of Gwen's who worked for the mayor, we were able to get our paperwork into the right hands far more quickly than we would have if we'd operated in a vacuum. If there was one thing we were good at, having had a ton of practice over the last few months, it was asking for help.

Once Monday rolled around, Ben made several trips to and from the DOB, and after pulling some strings, scored a meeting between himself; our architect, Jerry Caldari; and the Queens commissioner, Ira Gluckman, both of whom went to bat for us and helped us file the appropriate self-certification documents, obtaining the permit we needed. The violation was rescinded in thirty-six hours, but those thirty-six hours cost us, and not just the $5,000 in fines we paid, though that may have hurt more than anything. Ben was supposed to be catching up on rest that weekend in preparation for another big week but instead spent it on email and the phone, begging people to take his calls, printing papers, and helping me prepare a press statement for the inevitable Monday morning fallout. When the day finally came, I spent mine parroting the phrase "No further comment than that included in our statement," and Ben spent his down at the City Clerk's Office. As he walked out of there at midday on Tuesday, exhausted and $5,000 poorer for our troubles but with written permission in hand to continue working, his phone rang. It was the *Daily News*, calling to say they'd heard we got the order rescinded, and did he have a comment?

He hung up on them, scarfed down a slice of pizza across from the DOB office in Kew Gardens, and jumped on the train. No time for press, and not a moment to spare on celebration. We had to get back to work.

When we finally got the crane operators to return to the job after canceling on them with short notice and resumed work on Thursday of week two, things were a bit different. We didn't allow press on the roof anymore. Everyone wore hard hats, in spite of the heat. When our friend Jared showed up in flip-flops with a giant watermelon and pulled a machete out of his travel pack to cut it open, we told him to lose the knife and stay off the construction site with those open-toed shoes. We still laughed and cracked jokes as we ate that watermelon, but a shift had occurred. Until then, the entire project had seemed so utopian— magical, even: our eleventh-hour location score, the landlord's attentiveness as we signed a lease quickly enough to launch the project in time for the season, the outpouring of support and helping hands . . . Now we realized how tenuous it was. All eyes were on us, and one misstep could change the course of the farm's future—and ours along with it.

During the second week of craning soil, we worked hard. There were tense moments: a storm blowing in as we were near completion and the threat along with it of the crane guys canceling the remainder of the day, forcing us to hire them again for an additional day that we couldn't afford. And to add insult to injury, we had a DOB vehicle parked at the end of Standard Lane, the dead-end street on which we'd parked the crane, just sitting there watching our every move. But we completed the installation work in six days over the course of two weeks, hauling and shoveling out an average of sixty supersacks, or over 160,000 pounds of soil, for each day that we had the crane. After the last bag was lifted and the buggies were craned down to ground level, everyone collapsed in the shade of the water tower. It was dead silent, save for the rush of traffic below. Gwen passed out atop a trash bag of filter fabric scraps and irrigation line trimmings. Ben tiptoed away and started planting out tomatoes. A few weeks later the rows were dug, the seedlings were transplanted, and slowly, a farm began to take shape.

The shape the farm took was far more orderly than the installation had been. For all our talk of monstering, we didn't walk into the process of building the farm and planting it out blindly. While there were aspects of the installation for which we weren't totally prepared, there were far more that were strategic and deliberate. For starters, we had to actually plot out where everything would go—and what those things were.

One aspect of the start-up process that required some mental elbow grease was the bed layout. The bizarre shape of the flagship farm made it difficult to plan neat, tidy rows with consistently-sized beds. Having consistent bed sizes is a best practice that's taken for granted by most farmers: with uniformity, a farmer only has to do the math once. If we had beds equal to one another in size, we could calculate exactly how many ounces of fish emulsion we should order for six applications per season. We would be able to multiply the length of each row by the total number and know exactly how much irrigation drip tape to order. Harvest time and yields could be measured in a single unit. In other words, we could take some steps to control the chaos. But, alas, it was not to be. Our unconventional farm was quirky in every conceivable way.

So when we were laying out our first farm, we gave up on the luxury of uniformity and instead focused our energies on maximizing grow space, vacillating between long runs and short ones, debating which would allow us more room. We were fortunate to collaborate at this stage with our partner Jerry and his team at the architecture firm Bromley Caldari, who helpfully produced scaled plans of the roof, including all obstructions. Ultimately, the awkward shape of the roof informed our decision to dig short north-south beds perpendicular to the length of the building and bisected by the six-foot cart path down the center. The resulting design left us with about two dozen consistent beds out of two hundred; the remaining rows get incrementally longer as you make your way down the farm. If the beds weren't going to make our lives easier by being uniform, they could at least make our business more profitable by being as accommodating as space allowed!

The quirky bed dimensions made planning and record keeping more arduous than we'd have liked. Ben put a ton of time into calculating the area of our wonky rows, measuring each one out, and plugged the dimensions into spreadsheets during a time in which we were basically just treading water trying to keep up with the harvest.

To the casual observer, this might have seemed like more math than it was worth, but the time he spent up front saved our business countless hours of head scratching and number crunching in the field. And when you're on your farm looking at a long to-do list and the sun dropping lower in the sky by the moment, having to stop and look up proper plant spacing on your phone because you didn't figure it out earlier is a distraction you can't afford. That's why we take the time at the end of every single season, no matter how bone tired we are, to sit down and discuss what could be streamlined, what could work more efficiently. While the workload is still fresh in our minds, we look at any and all measures we can take to make our lives easier the following season. Whether it's a tool we need to purchase or an online platform for registering CSA members, there is always some system we can put in place to create order.

While too much planning can be a time suck, the right amount is essential to keeping the bedlam at bay. Anticipating your workload and building systems to stay organized in the craziest of months is essential to keeping a business running smoothly. To that end, we calculate and record just about every aspect of our business in Excel: the amount of seed we need to order, the number of seedling trays we should plant of each crop, and the yield we can get from each row into which those seedlings are planted. Even simple things like proper spacing of each crop is noted and uploaded to a shared drive, accessible to everyone on the farm.

In the case of laying out the flagship farm, we had planned the bed widths pretty deliberately. The layout was a key component in Ben's formula to eke out almost 50 percent more revenue per square foot than he had at Eagle Street. First off, he proposed a dramatic reduction of walkways and, more pertinent, a 25 percent increase in the widths of our beds over those at the Greenpoint roof. But not all that income was directly vegetable related: it also factored in alternative revenue streams like consulting, events, and a heavy emphasis on processed, shelf-stable foods like hot sauce and pickles. The formula also included an improved crop mix, and took into account an extended season achievable by starting seedlings and direct-sown crops earlier in the year.

Ben spent a tremendous amount of time on that crop list, carefully weighing how much square footage we should dedicate to each product. It's a tried-and-true best practice among farmers, and one that Richard Wiswall writes about at length in his book, *The Organic Farmer's Business Handbook*. We dedicated more space to the crops that had yielded large quantities of high-value vegetables at Eagle Street, and less to those that we knew to be loss leaders: the ones that took more time and more space and yielded a lower average per square foot.

Strategic product selection isn't unique to our line of work. Just as we quantify the value of each crop and plant what is most profitable, every business must make decisions about what to offer based on ROI. I saw this firsthand at the restaurants I worked for in my former career. Generally, a chef will base his or her menu on what sells the best—your steak, your salmon, your roast chicken—and order those things in bulk quantities to save on costs. At the same time, you want to offer variety and every chef has their favorite dishes to make. So you might offer something a little less practical but be strategic about it.

I remember a chef who kept a veal chop on the menu even though the meat was so expensive that, in spite of its hefty menu price, he barely made any money on it once he factored in the labor it took to prepare it and everything else that was plated with it. He couldn't charge much more for it without giving the tourist crowd at his midlevel restaurant a serious case of sticker shock. Instead, he only ordered a few portions to serve each night. Some people came in just for that dish, and the drinks and dessert they ordered along with it made up for the revenue he lost on the veal.

So when we planned how much of the farm to dedicate to

each type of vegetable, we weighed cut salad greens, kale, herbs, and tomatoes—the most profitable crops—more heavily than the summer squash that sprawled out and hogged space, or the carrots that took a leisurely eighty days to reach maturity. We planted the profitable items along with our veal chops— the obscure Italian chicories that chefs loved, or the fragrant herbs that drew people to the farm stand—in more sparing proportions.

By the time the farm was fully planted, it was July, and the installation, while only a few weeks behind us, felt like the distant past. The farm was thriving, and we had our hands full trying to harvest and sell everything we were growing. Every day was a new challenge: how to stake tomatoes so they held up to the fierce rooftop winds, or how to increase business to our farm stand. Every day we hustled harder, only to be met with a new challenge the next. Every day we showed up, and we monstered it.

Fast-forward to 2012, and we were at it again, planning an even more ambitious project atop a building almost twice as tall and nearly twice as large, with deeper soil at that. But this time, we were installing a farm on a roof under warranty and on city-owned land. This meant two things: because we were using government money and building on city property, there was a legal mandate in place to open the bidding process up to any and all contractors who qualified for the job, which prevents corrupt use of municipal funds—like hiring your uncle Larry's company to build a highway. The warranty, on the other hand, stipulated that only those applicators licensed by the company that had manufactured the membrane were eligible to apply. What this all boiled down to was that we were ineligible to do the job ourselves and wouldn't be lifting a finger to get the green roof materials and soil up to the roof. It also meant we couldn't ask for forgiveness instead of permission. Everything had to be planned and permitted ahead of time. This was a totally different ball game.

Our costs would increase as well. Between the third-party installers and the upgraded materials we were using, our budget inflated quickly to more than three times what the flagship farm had cost us. Fortunately, the installation was grant funded, so while we weren't keen on some of the materials costing more than they would have if we'd sourced them directly from the manufacturers with whom we enjoyed great relationships, we were breathing a sigh of relief at the idea of having the job done for us so we could focus on getting the flagship up and running for its third season.

That relief lasted about halfway through the month of March, at which point we were itching to start sowing seed but still looking at a bare roof. This time around, we had an entirely different installation method that we all thought would be a cinch: instead of using a crane to lift supersacks up to the roof, the soil manufacturer would dump the soil directly onto the pier, from whence we would transfer it to a smaller pile next to the building via a front loader with a hopper. From there, a truck with a kind of modified conveyor and chute would pump the soil into a huge tube and blow it up eleven stories where it would be deposited directly onto the green roof.

What is it they say about best-laid plans? That they explode in your face and leave you standing there wondering if it was a good idea to triple your payroll over the last year in anticipation of a second location as the calendar flips to April and you're still looking at a bare roof? Maybe that's not quite how Steinbeck would put it, but that's what we were thinking as the sun rose higher and the days grew longer and we still didn't have a farm. For starters, blowing soil and aggregate up to the height of our roof is a difficult endeavor that requires a delicate balance of material and air. Finding that perfect ratio took time, which we didn't have. To make matters worse, when the blower truck operator finally settled on an efficient ratio, we were delayed yet again because the truck couldn't blow wet soil, so we had to keep the pile tarped in anything more than a drizzle, and spring storms had arrived in full effect. For the next couple of weeks, it rained incessantly.

Once more, we found ourselves facing totally unanticipated speed bumps. We thought we'd planned this install so well, especially in comparison to the first time around. But no matter how much you plan, you can never truly know exactly how a project will unfold, and more often than not, your best course of action is to let go of that part of yourself that wants to control every aspect.

Once the weather dried out a bit, things really started coming along, and in a few weeks, we went from fretting over our bare roof to digging out rows. At this point, it was mid-May, and Ben and our farm manager, Matt, were following behind the applicators and their blower tubes—much to their chagrin—with our handmade dipstick and a couple of shovels, like flies trailing a horse in summer, already tunneling out the walkways as each section was being topped off.

We would start our installations earlier in the year if we could, but freezing conditions make that impossible. If blowing wet soil isn't doable, blowing frozen soil is a joke. To that end, we've come to count on a short first season for any major project we build. But once in a while, we actually get ahead of schedule. Smaller-scale projects are always completed in time, like the microfarm we installed atop our friend Carlos's restaurant, Rosemary's, in the spring of 2012. It took a team of five folks a day and a half. The building was only one story, so we engaged a boom truck equipped with a mini-crane, which lifted the sacks directly from the truck flatbed to the roof. The membrane was brand new and we used Enkadrain, a single-layer, roll-out green roof base with a monofilament drainage layer, which sped things along tremendously. In an ideal world, every roof we build out would be one or two stories tall, perfectly rectangular, and surrounded by forty feet of unobstructed paved access for a crane so that it could dump soil progressively in sections.

But we don't live in a perfect world, and as they say, perfection is the enemy of good. So if we want a better city, dotted with rooftop farms, we'll have to monster our way through some messy installs. And we're prepared. We've learned to start our seedlings off-site so we've got healthy transplants ready to go when our farms are eventually completed. We've learned to keep installations free of press and other distractions but also to budget for short seasons in our first year, just in case. And we've learned that, as challenging as installations may be, the real job comes afterward. If you think it's hard work to build a rooftop farm, try farming on one.

5

A WORK IN PROGRESS

Taking Stock and Creating Order

Now that we'd built the farm, we had to actually farm the roof. First, we'd had to prove the concept. Then once we'd built proof of the concept, we had to elevate it from the conceptual to the real. It's one thing to plan a hypothetical business, and another thing entirely to operate it. The former is based on projections, best guesses, and aspirations. The latter is about analyses, hard data, and coming to terms with reality. It's an ongoing undertaking. Farming is messy work. Nature has its own order, and it isn't particularly tidy. On any given day up on the roofs, we're faced with new challenges that interrupt anything resembling a routine. Fierce winds wrest plants from their stakes, blow straw used as mulch into neighboring walkways, and kick up soil everywhere. Someone's dirt-crusted pants got soaked as she rushed to seed a row before the rain hit, and they're now hanging to dry somewhere they shouldn't be. Flea beetles munch holes in the arugula till it looks like Swiss cheese. For anyone who thrives on organization and order, it's the stuff of nightmares.

Running a new business isn't any less chaotic. There's never enough time in the day, and when you do find a way to cram it all into your itinerary, something unexpected inevitably comes up that tears it all to shit. Your perfectly balanced budget didn't account for the machine that broke down and needs to be replaced, and your staffing schedule was a work of art, till your employee called in sick with the flu. It's always when you're running twenty minutes behind for a meeting you've been trying to get on the calendar for months that you get a call from some department official to tell you they're arriving for a surprise inspection, and maybe you get so flustered that you drop and shatter your phone. Sound like the worst day ever? Around here, we just call it a Tuesday.

As a small-business owner, you're the one accountable no matter what comes up. And when you have no idea how to solve whatever disaster is rearing its ugly head, the onus can be downright overwhelming, especially when you're a farmer and have to "manage" the vagaries of your environment. Eighty pounds of salad greens to pick before noon? How about some forty-mile-per-hour wind gusts that blow the leaves right out of your harvest bin? Spent three hours calling chefs and selling that bumper crop of tomatoes, did you? Too bad it decided to pelt down rain all night, splitting their skins and turning them into leaky bags of sauce.

Of course, mayhem isn't unique to farming. Every Web site designer has experienced technical difficulties just in time for launch day, and every restaurant owner has had a walk-in fridge burn out the morning of a reviewer's visit. The only certainty in small-business management is Murphy's Law.

There are a few things we've learned to do to help us handle the number of balls we're constantly juggling—in addition to the ones that are occasionally thrown at us. Our "just monster it" strategy was crucial to getting us through the install and early days, and there's still a good measure of monstering happening today, even all these years later. But as our business grew months and then seasons older, we had more than just monsters as our munition: we had experience. And any measure of success that we've achieved over the years has been a result of learning from our mistakes.

When you're planning your small business, some well-meaning person will advise you to expect the unexpected. There is nothing more infuriating than this meaningless, oxymoronic platitude. Perhaps a more accurate and helpful idiom might be to expect the unexpected thing to happen *again*, and to learn from it the first time around so it doesn't knock you off balance when it comes around a second time. We might not be able to anticipate what the next disaster will be, but we can learn from the last one the best way to handle the next one. Fool us once, shame on you; fool us again, and we should really have a contingency plan in place.

We've learned, for example, to design our operations as efficiently as possible. This might sound obvious, but it's amazing how easily you find yourself getting excited about ideas that might make your project more beautiful or unique. Yet if these ideas come at the expense of even five minutes of your time, you're doing yourself and your nascent business a major disservice. You've got to kill your darlings as soon as you see them for the precious flights of fancy that they are. When we first began laying out the flagship farm, we had a plan to incorporate every last mechanical obstruction on the roof into our design. It will be a new kind of urban permaculture, we exclaimed! We will utilize the resources of our own roof topography! We'll put heat-loving crops under heat-venting HVACs and moisture-seeking crops in the watershed! Those awkward corners that are all but unreachable on a daily basis are perfect for our long-lead crops, like melons and gourds! All shall live in harmony, whether natural or man-made!

This idealism lasted about half a season.

The reality is, those vents blowing warm air through the winter aren't consistent enough to keep tender young vegetables warm but are perfectly adequate in providing a winter safe haven for flea beetle larvae that would otherwise have frozen or starved to death. The hard-to-reach corners and condensate marshes provide the perfect growing conditions for the weeds we spend hours eradicating from our beds. They're also downright hard to navigate, and we quickly got sick of the hopping over, sidling around, tripping, cursing, toe stubbing, seed packet dropping, and cursing some more. When we designed the Navy Yard farm, we put a border of landscaping stone around all those pest-harboring mechanicals, and didn't waste money green roofing the hard-to-reach corners at all. Now when we see sites on which we're contemplating building a third location, we net out the square footage of any awkward bits and pieces and focus on only those areas where we can install large, equilateral tracts of farm area.

We still use the topographical features of the roof to inform our decisions about farming: we amend and water at the high points so that the pitch of the roof carries the nutrients downward. But we've given up on idealistic notions like using the warm air from an HVAC unit to heat our greenhouse. It's just too complicated to seal the plastic around the mechanicals and too space intensive to build one around it. When we strip away the romanticism—or rather, when we end a full day of work and the only item we've crossed off our punch list is "weed the southeast corner"—we realize just how much of a time suck this "harmoniousness" can be. And when there are a million disruptions breaking up your workflow to begin with, the best thing a new business owner can do is keep it simple. If an aspect of your plans doesn't positively correlate to your productivity, ax it.

There are some measures that seem more efficient on paper than they do in practice. Sometimes you have to work through a challenge in real time to understand how to optimize it. For example, when we began designing the flagship farm, part of Ben's plan to eke out extra growing space, and the revenue that came with it, was to significantly increase the width of each bed to five feet. Now, Ben and Gwen both happen to be quite tall and lanky, but I measure in at a mere five feet three inches, and when Ben raised this plan to the group, I was quick to point out the injustice. I spent many a morning post-harvest grumbling that I could have filled my bins faster if I'd been able to reach the whole way across the bed, and many an afternoon emerging from a row of Sun Golds with tomato tar all over my scowling face from climbing inside the thicket to trellis the center plants.

Finally, after two seasons of sore backs, the taller members of the team relented—the beds were too wide. And not just for us shorties: five-foot beds also didn't make sense for some of our crops. For our deeper-rooted varieties, like bushy eggplants or tall tomatoes, it wasn't quite enough space for three rows of plants but a waste of space with only two. So when I was done gloating, we set out with shovels and began the incredibly laborious task of digging out and reshaping every single bed—all

120 of them—into 200. To make up for the space we lost by adding so many walkways, we reduced those walkways from eighteen inches to sixteen inches. The whole project took a solid week of everyone pitching in one spring before the farm was planted out. It was hard, tedious work, but three months later, when we were harvesting, we looked back on it without an ounce of regret.

Obviously we try to avoid redesigning our farms after building them, so after our trial-by-fire experience at the flagship farm, we've learned to put a lot of time into imagining ourselves in the space. When we were designing our second farm at the Brooklyn Navy Yard, we thought long and hard about where the points of entry were and how close the wash and pack stations could be to the elevator. The egress point should be close to the walk-in cooler, which of course should be close to the wash station, which of course should be in the shade. Any extra minute it takes to walk from the wash station to the cooler might seem negligible, but when your crew makes that trip thousands of times during a season, often carrying a stack of packed harvest bins loaded with heavy carrots and cucumbers, you realize you're hemorrhaging efficiency. Strategically designing shortcuts into a business from the outset means working smarter, not harder.

Just as we're always thinking about how our space can improve the efficiency of our labor practices, we're also trying to make sure the products of our work are valued as highly as they can be, which means deriving as much profit from our crops as possible. When we planned the flagship farm, we dedicated more space to profitable greens, herbs, and tomatoes and less to those popular but low-value items that draw bodies to our farm stand or entice our CSA members to reenroll for the following season. We had to: there's not much room for whimsy on the farm.

Ben's cucuzza squash project is a prime example. Our friend and early customer Giuseppe mentioned that he would love to get his hands on some of the rare Italian delicacies, and we agreed to grow them. They were a hoot to see, and people loved to have their photos taken with the three-foot-long curved cucurbits at our market table. But we're not running a photobooth business, we're selling vegetables, and they took more time and space to grow than we could afford. They simply weren't keeping the lights on.

But while we've always understood that squash in general isn't a particularly profitable crop, it wasn't just a hunch that cucuzzas were a drag on our bottom line. We know exactly how much money those cucuzzas brought in per square foot because Ben took the time to track their data and create an enterprise budget for them. An enterprise budget is an important bookkeeping practice for farmers. It takes into account the profit and loss for each crop or project individually rather than the farm as a whole (once again, Richard Wiswall's *The Organic Farmer's Business Handbook* is an excellent resource on this topic). So rather than just calculating the price per square foot of a given crop, a well-designed enterprise budget also factors in the cost of seed and fertilizer, the value of the labor required to cultivate the crop to maturity, and any packaging materials, such as plastic cartons, pint containers, or rubber bands for bunching.

Ben was methodical about keeping data for each of the crops that we grew, especially in our first couple of seasons. Once we set up QuickBooks, a digital bookkeeping service, the tracking process became considerably more streamlined, but even before we did so, Ben made the time to plug data from each big wholesale harvest or market into a spreadsheet. At the end of the season, we could compare the square footage we'd planted of each crop to the date we'd planted it, the date we began harvesting it, how many pounds we harvested, and how much money it had brought in. If we dedicated sixty square feet to cucuzzas, and it took three months, a third of the season, to reach maturity but only yielded ten pounds at $4 a pound, then we earned a scant $2 per foot on those squash over the course of the season. And that $2 per foot was only achievable if we hustled to get that space planted during the other two-thirds of the growing season, leaving little time for bed prep, not to mention the amount of labor that squash requires to trellis, the pests they harbor, and so on. Our goal for the farm that first year was $3 a foot, and has risen steadily since as we've become more profitable; cucuzzas weren't even close to hitting our goal.

Look, we know it's fun to grow squash. We love squash!

But if you can't pay rent growing squash, you simply cannot grow squash. And you'll never know if squash pays the rent unless you're running the numbers. It might seem intuitive for a farmer to base success on how healthy, delicious, or popular their crop is rather than factoring in the cost of seed, fertilizer, and labor that goes into it, but it's not an accurate picture of a business's profitability. That said, a chef might be more loyal to a farmer who can grow him the crop he loves, so it might be necessary to hook an account with a cucuzza so as to sell them other more profitable greens. But that doesn't mean we should lose money on the cucuzzas. If Giuseppe really wanted us to grow them, and we really wanted to make at least $3 per square foot on them—maybe even slightly more, since they were a labor-intensive crop to grow—we would have to charge him $7 a pound for his goofy gourds. If he was willing to pay that much, we would happily undertake the project; otherwise, it just wasn't a good fit for our farm. As a small-business operator himself, Giuseppe is sympathetic to our focus on the bottom line, and even if he's not willing to shell out, he won't be offended by us asking for what we need to make the endeavor worthwhile.

It doesn't matter if you're growing squash or building bicycles, if you don't have an enterprise budget for each product you sell, you don't have a grip on your business. We believe that to run a profitable farm only one thing is as urgent as the immediate needs of the plants, and that's data. Like a growing number of small-scale farmers working today, we embrace the philosophy that farming should be profitable, and a farmer can only determine the profitability of a given enterprise if she actually knows what its revenues and expenses are. This is true of every industry. Know what resources your products require, and what value they bring to the table. It better be a favorable ratio, or that product is a loss leader—and there's no room for loss leaders in a brand-new small business that is trying to make a name for itself. Every vegetable we grow requires a certain amount of our resources, and if we can't measure that against the revenue it generates, then we'll never know whether it's truly a success. The trick is to identify which areas of our business are the real winners and eliminate any nonessential tasks that don't directly generate revenue.

Understanding which tasks are essential can be a bit tricky when you're surrounded by urgency and everyone wants a piece of you. Even the profit-minded farmer will find that midseason, when she is elbow deep in ripe tomatoes with a short shelf life and sees more fruit on the vines blushing deeper with every passing moment, it can seem counterintuitive to stop picking or making deliveries for even the few moments it takes to record the last couple of sales or the yields of one variety versus another. But these are the crucial data points that can determine whether tomatoes are a worthwhile crop on her farm, and if they are, how she can pull her net up a few percentage points next season.

We're certainly not the first farmers to value data. Farmers have been tracking planting dates, harvesting dates, yields, weather fluctuations, and so on for as long as humans have been farming. Hell, you can walk into many an eighteenth-century barn and find crop lists and hash marks scratched into the walls in shorthand legible only to some long-gone author. But if our conversations with fellow small producers are any indication, the profitability philosophy as a guiding principle is gaining more and more traction, and thanks to experts like Richard Wiswall, our industry is quickly putting aside the idea that farming is a trade for the rural poor or that making money is only for capitalist pigs. Wiswall makes a case that farmers can make a very comfortable living growing and selling food, as long as they are shrewd.

More often than not, it's not the farmers who play down the work required on the back end to operate profitably. On the contrary, it's the desk jockeys—people working in media or tech start-ups—who make comments about how nice it must be to not have to sit in front of a computer crunching numbers. One of our least favorite comments, which we must hear once a day in autumn, is "Wow, it must be nice to have your whole winter off." Meanwhile, our chief financial officer, Melissa, who spends the summer and fall chasing down unpaid invoices and balancing the farm's books, as well as helping to manage projects across departments and keeping us all organized, is busiest just as production on the farm begins to slow down. December and January are her craziest months as she reconciles expenses across categories, gets everyone paid, and sends off the books to our tax preparer. As Ben likes to say, "Winter is when we make our money," when we look hard at our business, make improvements on the last season, and plan the next one. Executing the plan during the growing season is hard work, sure, but that's the fun part. The real meat of what we do happens at a desk in winter.

It's a hard truth to impart on those eager to leave six-figure-salaried office jobs in fluorescent-lit cubicles for the romance of working the land. We take no pleasure in dashing quixotic dreams with QuickBooks realities. Or, at least, not as much pleasure as Joel Salatin seems to take. The farmer made famous by Michael Pollan's *Omnivore's Dilemma* and steward of the now-famous Polyface Farm, Salatin will baffle anyone who has trouble reconciling the idea of capitalism with environmentalism. As uncompromising as his green politics are, the self-proclaimed "Christian libertarian environmentalist capitalist lunatic" never misses an opportunity to impress upon his readers that farming is a business. As he says in his book *You Can Farm: The Entrepreneur's Guide to Start and Succeed in a Farming Enterprise*:

> While it's true farming is about glorious sunsets, newborn lambs gamboling in the clover, frost on the pumpkin, and snow in the pines at Christmas, it is also about money. It is about the harsh discipline of self-employment. It is about

capital allocation and learning not to be cheap but "tight." [. . .] If these latter "business" things do not excite and intrigue you as much as that thought of the sunset, I recommend you don't try to farm for a living.

Not cheap but "tight." We also like the term "scrappy." "Resourceful" and "frugal" work, too. We walked into our business with this principle in mind above all else: an urban farm can be profitable or it will go out of business. The truth is, in the early years right after we started the farm, we were beyond shrewd; we were downright cheap! We didn't have much of a choice because we didn't have any money! We were so cheap that when the fierce rooftop winds began blowing our irrigation lines around atop the beds, crushing tender young shoots in the process, we went to a dry cleaner and got a bunch of coat hangers. We spent half a day and tore our hands up untwisting them, cutting them to size, and bending them into shape just to save the $12 we would have otherwise spent on irrigation staples. We should have just spent the money, of course. The time we spent was worth more than the dollars we saved.

We didn't learn right away to value our time. It's not easy as a small-business operator. You're the variable. You're the one element over which you have total control. You can't make the weather cooperate, and you can't speed up the shipment of seeds, but you can put in a sixteen-hour day to catch up when the seeds show up late and there are gale force winds that prevent you from getting them in for two days. You are your own most precious resource. But if you push yourself too hard, you destroy that resource. These days, while we're not exactly punching out at five o'clock to hit the local bar for happy hour, we have become better at valuing ourselves and imposing limits on what we can realistically get done. And sometimes when you step back to look at the big picture, the things you determine to be priorities are not what you would expect: getting the irrigation lines stapled down might seem crucial, until you slice through your hand with a wire hanger in the process of doing it and lose the use of that hand for a week while the stitches heal. Then you really wish you'd ponied up the cash for real staples, or just let the wind whip the lines around and destroy a hundred dollars' worth of crops.

But it can be tough to see the forest for the trees when you're as busy as a brand-new business operator. When we built the Navy Yard farm in the spring of 2012, we neglected the flagship farm badly. We planted it from parapet wall to wall, and eked out a laudable harvest each week, but we were so focused on getting the new location set up that we didn't spend enough time weeding and adding amendments like compost. As a result, our crops the following season suffered from poor nutrition and unhealthy competition. We're still battling a weed population at the flagship farm that grew strong and prolific in that hectic season. If we'd hired someone to come up and weed for a day or two each week, we would have made the money back in the difference of productivity in the years to follow.

It was a hard lesson to learn but one that we'll never forget: there are today's priorities, and tomorrow's, and finding the balance is an art that takes time. It might be as simple as adding one thing to your punch list each day that will improve your business six months from now, a year from now, a decade in the future. It's hard to see past the end of any given day sometimes, but it's important even in those busy times to make sure you're evaluating the long-term health of a business. Rather than just pouring energies into getting through the day-to-day, a smart operator is making time to look at the following year, three years, even five years down the line. When you think you don't have thirty seconds to spare, forcing yourself to slow down and place your day in the context of that week, that month, that year, and beyond is the best way to save yourself time down the road.

Sometimes it's hard to determine just what is best for the business. The high-level decisions we treat with as much thoughtfulness and analysis as possible, but for smaller day-to-day decisions, we've learned to make a choice and live with it. Spring is all about quick decision making. We start seeding cold-weather crops like radishes, turnips, and snap peas as soon as the ground is soft enough to work. A few weeks later, once we're reasonably certain we're out of danger of a hard frost, we'll begin transplanting cold-hardy seedlings—the kale, chard, and onions. But best-laid plans are often mocked by nature, who has her own agenda. In 2014, the ground softened up in early April. We planted row upon row of salad greens, only to watch them all stiffen in shock as a late-season snowstorm struck at the end of the month. Most of them recovered—eventually. But the greens we planted a few days after the storm ended up outpacing their frost-bitten predecessors, which went in the ground over two weeks before them.

Radishes and snap peas are another annual wager each spring. Plant them early enough and harvest a crop before anyone else, and you'll have chefs begging you for an order and farm-stand customers lining up at your stall. But a late, prolonged frost of a couple of days will freeze the early seedlings, and they'll rot as they thaw. It's a gambler's game, farming. You can check ten different weather apps and read the almanac till your eyes cross, but no one knows with any real certainty when she antes up those first spring crops whether she's about to be dealt a royal flush of five straight sixty-degree sunny days or a late cold front that will blow through and clear the pot.

The most dangerous thing about the uncertainty of spring plantings is that it leads to equivocation, and equivocation wastes time. Ask any small-business operator what she's short on, and there's a damn good chance she'll tell you she could use a few more hours in the day. So if analysis paralysis wastes even fifteen minutes of our time as we vacillate between whether to sow some snap peas or wait another couple of days, we're losing our most precious resource. Often, it pays to just make a call.

Having to make a choice can leave us dizzy, and the sense that we've made the wrong choice can rob us of coveted sleep at night. The only way to get through it without completely losing your mind is to make peace with imperfection. I once knew a carpenter who would reassure his team, when they didn't finish their assigned tasks for the day, "Relax, it's not produce. It doesn't go bad." Unfortunately, that's not a principle we can apply to our business. From last frost to first frost, farming is urgent work. Everything needs to get done now, if it's not already too late. And yet, it's not uncommon to hear Ben console an apologetic farmhand with a similar sentiment: "It's OK. At the end of the day, it's just food."

Which is not to say we don't take our crops seriously, and we've all gotten bent out of shape about a stupid mistake that cost us an order. But we try to embrace the mayhem of our business. It's the only way to manage it. If you try to control it, you become a disaster forecaster, and the energy you would spend getting things done and crossing them off your punch list is wasted on creating contingency plans you may never use. And if you let it get under your skin, you may as well quit right now.

Our farms are far from perfect, and we've learned to live with the frustrations. As we rack up seasons on the roofs, we become better at understanding our growing conditions, and there's one feature that has become abundantly clear to us over the years: our soil dries out faster than it should. Our average particle size is fairly large, which gives our growing medium unusual porosity. Tiny pockets of air between the small stones create space for water to flow through, and once that water has drained, places for air to collect and dry out the surrounding particles. And there lies the double-edged sword of drainage: on the one hand, it's essential to farming on a rooftop. Sure, the soil needs to be super well drained in order for the roof not to fill up like a bathtub and collapse under the weight, but it also makes it very difficult to keep the soil moist, especially considering how much airflow the shallow beds get in our windy conditions.

Excessive drainage also means you risk flushing nutrients out of your soil every time it rains heavily. In order to understand the idiosyncrasies of our soil, here's a quick (and unforgivably reductionist) primer on how soil works: topsoil is full of nutrients that come from decaying organic matter, minerals in rainfall, rocks, etc. Healthy dirt is also inhabited by a community of microorganisms that eat those nutrients and poop them out in a form that is more accessible to plants. The plants feast on certain sets of nutrients that they need most to grow, and in a natural environment, those plants eventually die, shedding foliage that decays and helps replenish the nutrients in the soil. When rainfall drains through topsoil, it flushes some of the nutrients that aren't being tied up by microorganisms or used up by plants into the subsoil, where they remain accessible to deeper-rooted plants and living organisms.

On a farm where plants are removed from the ground and their decaying tissue isn't left to replenish soil, nutrients are often replaced by adding compost and "amendments," or fertilizers. Most amendments are a blend of nitrogen (N), phosphorus (P), and potassium (K), but some are straight nitrogen, which is the single most important element in growing edible food plants.

On a farm with healthy soil that sees lots of microbial action, the nitrifying bacteria present in populous microbial communities will break down the strong triple bonds of nitrogen and digest it into its simpler forms—nitrites and nitrates—which plants will suck up hungrily, leaving only small amounts to drain into the subsoil or evaporate into the atmosphere. For most of human history, creating a favorable environment for these microbes was the prevailing method of managing soil and farming successfully.

Then the green revolution happened, and scientists discovered a way to manufacture nitrates synthetically. The discovery marked a huge advancement for farming. Now nitrogen could be made immediately available to plants regardless of the health of a soil's microbial community. Unfortunately, synthesizing this fertilizer requires converting atmospheric nitrogen into plant-accessible forms by burning large amounts of fossil fuels. In our attempt to create one resource, we've exploited another, which has proven to be less profuse than we ever could have imagined. There was another long-term effect of synthetic fertilization: nitrates of any provenance, synthetic or natural, are extremely mobile and hard to pin down. Their molecular structure will evolve and change, at which point they can be absorbed quickly and easily into the atmosphere and dissolved into runoff. While synthetic fertilizers eliminate the need for nitrifying bacteria, they don't eliminate the need for any microbial life whatsoever.

Applications of synthetic nitrogen are often accompanied by applications of chemical pesticides and fungicides, and the practice of deep tilling, all of which damage soil structure. These procedures are tantamount to napalming a city and then bulldozing it. The system poisons the microbial communities and then destroys their homes. Without the microbial infrastructure necessary to house nitrates and release them to plants more gradually, chemically reliant systems depend on applying more synthetic fertilizers than the plants actually need to make up for what is lost during major rain events. While the crops themselves will take up a certain amount—60 percent is generally accepted as efficient—the rest is released into our environment, polluting our air and draining into the subsoil.

Molly Culver, an urban farmer and "growing soils" teacher at

Farm School NYC refers to the role that synthetic nitrogen plays as "the cheap but essential accomplice to an industrial farm's pro-crop fertility plan." As she explained in an email to me:

> A pro-microbe soil fertility plan, the backbone of organic and sustainable farming, favors a focus on diverse yet measured organic matter incorporation, minimized soil disturbance and tillage, and crop rotation—the basic requirements for a diverse and abundant microbe population—and their ability to digest and convert nutrients into plant-available forms.

Determined to farm organically, we have always added as much finished compost to our soil as possible in an attempt to make our ecosystem attractive to the microbial community. And we've planted cover crops in winter to manage nutrient leeching caused by the runoff of melting snowpack. We apply fish fertilizer, an organic amendment made with the liquefied "gully" of fish: the 70 percent of its bones, head, scales, and guts left over after the fillet has been cut and removed. These are broad-spectrum amendments, and applying them regularly is a farmer's best chance of throwing a party to which the microbial community wants to come. In our first year, the farm was so fecund, we struggled to sell crops as quickly as we grew them.

But then, as early as our second season farming the flagship roof, we noticed something disturbing: the beets wouldn't grow.

Their leaves would grow, but the roots themselves were small and hard as rocks. Ah, it must be the soil depth, we figured consolingly, and perhaps a bit naively, given the fact that they'd grown just fine the year prior. When the arugula started suffering, we knew our soil-depth theory was wishful thinking. We chastised ourselves for spending too much time planning the Navy Yard and not enough time amending our soil with compost applications. We were growing too much too densely for the nutrients we had available, and we weren't replacing them efficiently enough, we figured. We doubled down on our compost program, and built a forced-air system that speeds up decomposition by shooting jets of oxygen through our compost for roughly thirty seconds every thirty minutes. We even bought twenty yards of finished compost from an organic supplier nearby, dumping it in the loading dock of the building and shoveling it into five-gallon buckets, then ferrying those up the elevator to the roof.

We were deep in the design phase of the Navy Yard farm at this point, and Ben wisely reached out to Joe DiNorscia, a founding member of Rooflite, the company that manufactures our soil, to ask if we could increase the ratio of organic matter to lightweight stones in the Rooflite blend we'd be using at the new farm. Organic matter covers all the nonrock and mineral components of soil: basically anything that's living, or was at one point in time—bugs, wood, fungi, etc.—and though it only makes up a small percent of topsoil, it is responsible for most of its nutrients. Joe, with his background in farming, was immediately sympathetic to Ben's request and, determined to find a solution, looped in Rooflite's soil scientist.

But the regulating bodies that certify green roof medium have certain weight and porosity standards, to limit liability on their end and to differentiate their product from standard landscaping soil. At first it appeared that everyone's hands were tied, and we were stuck with the original blend. But Ben persevered, and with the support of Joe and their fellow dirt nerds at Rooflite, the company agreed to increase the organic matter in our growing medium by 50 percent. The new and improved "Intensive Ag" blend would be marketed specifically for growing nutrient-greedy edibles on rooftops or other areas with low weight ratings, like terrace planters. And when we saw the first crop of plants emerge at the Navy Yard, we were certain we had nipped the issue in the bud. They were monstrous! State fair winners down to the last! Heads of lettuce twice the size of our faces! Chard leaves as long as our forearms! Hallelujah! we thought to ourselves.

One summer day in 2014, in the twenty-seventh month of cultivating crops on the roof at the Navy Yard, Ben and our farm manager, Matt, were walking the rows together and noticed, with a gut-sinking sense of dread, a familiar sight: the arugula was turning purple. Some leaves just had a tinge of it creeping along the center veins; others were washed with a mauve tone across the entire tissue. The more purple the leaves, the more stunted their growth. Mostly, they looked a lot like the purple leaves we'd seen at the flagship farm two years before. We couldn't just give up on growing it; it's one of our most profitable crops, and a favorite among chefs for the particularly spicy bouquet it develops on our farm.

Frustrated to see the problem he thought we'd solved cropping back up again and faced with standing orders we couldn't come close to filling, Ben broke out the big guns and sent a photo, along with a brief note, to farmer Eliot Coleman. Coleman is one of the foremost organic growers, teachers, researchers, policy advisors, and tool developers in the trade (he's the man responsible for the precision seeder and the bed roller that we use). Ben had met him while visiting his farm in Maine a few months prior, and he had saved his email address for a critical situation just like this one.

Coleman thought the problem looked like a lack of nitrogen and proposed we test that hypothesis by digging trenches and using different soils—a high-grade potting mix, pure finished compost, and our own blend—side by side in the same bed and planting a row of arugula in each. We loved the idea—it was in keeping with everything we'd learned about collecting data on our operations—and implemented it right away, but it would take weeks to determine the results, which potentially meant losing our whole crop in the meantime.

Coleman wasn't the only trick up our sleeve, and Ben called as many farmer friends as he could in the weeks that followed.

Joe DiNorscia also pointed to nitrogen and, confident that the Intensive Ag blend should still hold sufficient nutrients after only two seasons of cultivation, suggested sampling the plant tissue to determine whether the issue was a lack of nitrogen in the soil or if it was present but inaccessible to the crops.

Finally, a fellow farmer named Curtis Stone, who has a ground-level urban farm business up in Canada not dissimilar to ours, suggested we apply a nitrogen-only fertilizer rather than the broad-spectrum N-P-K fish fertilizer we had been using. He liked blood and feather meal in particular, two great options for organic growers (though the blood meal can stink a bit). And what do you know: the beds on which we threw down these amendments came in looking much healthier. But just as we began breathing easy again, our tissue samples came back. The results only deepened the Mystery of the Purple Arugula: we had more than enough nitrogen in the plant tissue of the crappy arugula. So what the hell was going on with our farm?

A few months before all this soil business began, we had received a call from a scientist at Cornell named Thomas Whitlow, who had conducted the air quality tests at the flagship farm the year prior. He had a bright young PhD candidate on his research team who was interested in conducting a study of the farm. They had secured funding for three years of data collection and analysis that covered everything from weather stations to moisture sensors. That kind of information was exactly what we needed, so we agreed to take him on. And that's how we came to know Yoshiki Harada.

After a brief email intro, Ben set a date to meet Yoshi, as he calls himself, at the Navy Yard farm in the late winter of 2014. When the date arrived, Ben stood waiting down on the loading dock for Yoshi, whose picture he had never seen. It was early, and the farm was still pretty quiet. There was only one other soul around, some utilities official, Ben supposed, from Con Edison or maybe some other agency, wearing a neon vest with reflective strips, the kind that maintenance workers don so they're especially visible to oncoming traffic and trains. After a few minutes of waiting around, Ben became restless and decided to call Yoshi to see where he was. He dialed the number and heard a ringing—not just at the other end of the line but from the pocket of the maintenance worker standing to his left! As the two shook hands, Ben took in the man standing before him. He had at least four Sharpies in his chest pocket, and in the pocket beneath that, a sizable dry-erase board. He looked like he was about sixteen years old, and had a smile that could melt ice. Ben knew immediately that he would like Yoshi, and was expecting great things from the Harvard grad who had come so highly recommended. He was further impressed when they got upstairs, sat down in the office, and Yoshi unrolled a huge printout of a Google satellite image of the farm. This guy came prepared.

In the months that followed, Yoshi proved to fit right into our quirky little farmily, though he couldn't have looked more out of place. He had two outfits: the reflective gear he'd worn that wintry day in early spring, and a summer uniform that consisted of a black T-shirt, black jeans, a black belt, black socks, and black shoes. As we later learned, his brother sent the shirts from Japan, and he has a closet full of them. No matter how hot it was, he was faithful to his head-to-toe black attire. With twin master's degrees in urban engineering and landscape architecture, he is clearly committed to his work, though it's a bit unclear what spurred Yoshi's choice to study ecology in the first place. For starters, he admits freely that he hates nature. And who could blame him; nature doesn't appear to have any love for the man himself. No less than three bees stung Yoshi in the first weeks of his research, while the rest of us went unmolested. Yet he persevered, arriving each day with his tool belt of pliers and wire cutters, a package of zip ties tucked into his pocket, scrambling up ladder after ladder to attach satellite dishes to bulkheads from which his data would be sent wirelessly up to Cornell headquarters.

At the time of writing, it has been a year since Yoshi began studying our farm, and already the data he's collected has proven invaluable. While we're endlessly grateful to our fellow farmers for the wisdom and insight they have so generously shared with us over the years, never too busy to take a call or return an email from a young grower facing a new challenge, nobody has ever farmed in conditions identical to ours. No one has ever grown edible crops in the man-made ecosystem of a rooftop farm. Ben's knowledge and curiosity brought us further than many expected, but in order to keep growing our business and the soil rooftop farming model, we have a lot of information yet to collect.

Partnering with academic institutions is time-consuming. Matt spent countless hours during the 2014 growing season snipping leaves and overnighting them to Cornell's labs for Yoshi to analyze. Ben has spent even more time digging through emails for an old document that might be helpful to forward along to Yoshi and his team, or making introductions between them and the soil architects at Rooflite so they can compare notes on the original soil composition versus the current nutrient levels. But if we've learned anything over the years, it's that information is power. And no matter how irrelevant all this busywork seems in the face of a huge, imminent tomato harvest, the single most important thing we harvest on our farm is data.

For those of you who are anxious to know what happened with the purple arugula, the results of the tissue samples came back and seemed to solve the mystery: it was a potassium deficiency. Potassium is extremely soluble and mobile. It is also responsible for generating new cell growth, which makes sampling tissue all the more complicated, and potentially misleading; since these leaves are deficient in potassium, they grow less, which may mean the nutrients that are present are packed into a smaller space. So while it might appear that we have sufficient nitrogen, in fact, it might just be less widely distributed across fewer cells, thereby artificially elevating the levels read by the test. That would certainly explain why our applications of nitrogen-only amendments improved the quality of the arugula.

Also, it's likely that our nitrogen levels spike and drop dramatically as we add compost and organic fertilizers—along with our potassium and phosphorous levels, too—and that it's just really difficult to obtain an accurate reading. With that in mind, we balance our reliance on these tests with our powers of observation and our best understanding of our farm. One thing that's undeniably apparent is that we're losing nutrients down the drain—literally.

That right there is the paradox of the green roof farm: we slow down the rate at which rainfall passes through our farm, allowing the sewer systems to process peak flow rainfall before our runoff enters those subterranean pipes, thus reducing the amount of combined sewage overflow here in New York City. Yet all that water steals our nutrients much faster than it would if more moisture stayed in the system. The very climate feature that makes green roofs valuable simultaneously makes us vulnerable. The more valuable we become—that is, the more it rains heavily in our city—the more our soil is robbed of nutrients and the greater our vulnerability.

It's possible that the lessons we learn as we continue to study our unique conditions will have an impact on not just our business but on other on-structure landscapes, such as the High Line here in New York City and the trees planted along the sidewalk. It's possible that, as climate change flips the script across the globe, Yoshi's findings and the techniques we adapt on our roofs may be applicable to ground-level farms. As regions of our planet heat up and dry out, our findings may contribute to a growing body of research on how to manage ground-level soil in hotter, drier conditions. Even heavier snowpack—and resulting melt—may cause nutrient leeching and could have an impact on the quality of soil in regions now experiencing heavier winter precipitation.

Regardless, we know we've got an uphill battle ahead of us. We are determined to do what it takes to make our farm as sustainable and operational as possible. For us, there is no alternative. What are we going to do, throw up our hands and walk away from the business we've worked so hard to build? No, our little patches of rooftop soil are all we've got to work with, and they need to work hard. It is our job to manage them as faithfully as we can. That means continuing to arm ourselves with as much information as possible. So in addition to farmers, we've become research scientists, detectives, and regulars at the post office from which we dispatch weekly samples to Cornell's labs. But we never let these secondary and tertiary roles eclipse our primary goal. Most days, we keep our heads down, work hard, and accept that ours is not a perfect operation. We say it over and over again when we get frustrated: perfection is the enemy of good, and done is better than perfect.

The beautiful thing about farming is that you get a bit of a do-over every spring. Farmer Annie Novak, with whom Ben opened Eagle Street Rooftop Farm, calls it the "annual forgiveness of agriculture." Building healthy soil is an ongoing project, but most of our operations are temporal, and each spring, we have an opportunity to improve them: new CSA members to feed, new crops to try, sometimes even a new roof to transform into a farm. Not all businesses are as seasonal, but there's always opportunity for improvement, no matter how consistent an organization's operations are. Every operator should find a time to step back and look at the work she's done, and the better a company's record-keeping practices are, the more useful this reflection will be.

The trick is not to let the imperfections discourage you. It can be easy to get down on yourself for failing at one aspect of what you do, but if it distracts you from doing something else well, or figuring out how to be better at the things with which you struggle, your business will never move forward. We strive to be better, and that means being critical of ourselves and practical when it comes to how we spend our time and resources.

But it also means recognizing that trial-and-error will always be a part of any innovative business, and forgiving ourselves for the mistakes we make. As long as we learn from them, we can consider those mistakes growing pains, and see them as steps toward a healthier business rather than steps away from perfection.

It also helps immeasurably that we're not working in a vacuum. It can be tough to be objective about your own work. We're fortunate to have a diverse team, and one that's grown more so over the years as we hire additional staff and grow our business, because everyone has different perspectives, different areas of the farm for which they seek perfection. We are in awe of sole proprietors, but we don't envy them. Having one another to turn to when we struggle with a particular endeavor has helped our business become stronger. We make one another accountable, and we help one another be clear-eyed. It's this shared commitment—to the farm and to one another—that allows our business to truly thrive and grow year to year.

6

WE ARE FARMILY

Growing Our Team

I f you'd told any of us when we started Brooklyn Grange that forming an LLC with people is basically tantamount to becoming a family, we might not have signed the operating agreement. We're all incredibly different people, with totally divergent styles of doing business. Sometimes it seems that the only characteristics we share are that we're fiercely opinionated and bullishly willful. But the truth is, we share something far more important than closely held beliefs: we respect one another. We all realize the farm wouldn't be what it is without the contributions each of us has made, and it's that shared commitment and mutual trust that makes us work well as a team—or as we like to call ourselves, a farmily.

When we were planning the farm, we were a team of five:

Ben, Gwen, myself, Chris, and Brandon. Once the farm was built, Chris and Brandon had to return to running Roberta's, which had become something of a critical hit and was expanding rapidly to meet the growing demand of the community. And besides, Chris had always been clear that he was planning on taking a step back once we were up and running, as Roberta's kept him plenty busy, and he was less interested in operating the farm than he was in getting the project off the ground. Some folks like making deals and starting projects, others are more day-to-day operations types; Chris was definitely the former. But even though the two aren't involved in managing the business, Chris and Brandon have remained in our orbit as advisors, and the restaurant is a valuable account for us.

After the Roberta's boys departed, Ben, Gwen, and I divvied up operational responsibilities and put a labor plan into action. Ben was our head farmer and president of the company; I handled communications, public programming, and events (basically, external affairs); and Gwen oversaw facilities, office management, and accounting—the latter responsibility being one she took on gamely, if not quite enthusiastically. She wasn't exactly thrilled to keep spreadsheets of our financials, set up a bank account, or deposit checks every week, but someone had to do it, and we didn't have the budget to hire anyone. When you're starting a business, there are a million things that need to get done. To that end, the aforementioned "job duties" didn't even begin to cover the range of activities for which each of us was responsible. Gwen and I were out in the field, seeding and harvesting with Ben, on a daily basis. We all manned the farmer's market tables, and Gwen ran deliveries in her pickup truck from time to time. Ben helped Gwen with accounting, keeping a close eye on the books, invoicing all the sales, and chasing down outstanding debts in person when needed. We all wore a lot of hats, and still do. The phrase "That's not my job" never entered our lexicon.

Unfortunately, we didn't have room in the budget for Gwen or me to draw a salary—which we had known heading into the enterprise. We had financed a lot of the materials needed to build the farm, which still needed to be paid off, plus we weren't generating much revenue for the first couple of months while we waited for our first succession of crops to grow. Additionally, *someone* needed to be on salary, to be responsible for the business all day, every day, without the distractions of another job. And that person was Ben, who spent every waking hour— including many during which he should have been asleep—at the farm. Without the time to take another job to support himself, he would need to be compensated at least enough to pay his rent and feed and clothe himself.

And that pretty much capped our operating budget for the first two years: rent, insurance, loan repayments, seeds, and Ben. So Gwen and I did what many farmers—and many new business owners—do to make ends meet: we maintained jobs off the farm. Gwen was employed as the grower at Roberta's, which made sense because she could apply a certain economy of scale to her work. Ordering supplies for one farm? Why not order them for both, save on the shipping, and reimburse the entity that paid the total for the half going elsewhere?

My own job made slightly less sense. I was a bartender at my former boss's restaurant, a little Italian osteria downtown. I would head up to the farm in the morning; harvest an order with Ben and Gwen; then wash, pack, and invoice it; hose myself off; and haul the whole stack of bins into the subway, where I'd get all sorts of weird looks from my fellow straphangers. I'd get to the restaurant and take the veggies straight down to the walk-in refrigerator, tie on my apron, and spend the next six or seven hours slinging drinks and serving up the greens we'd picked earlier that day. I'd arrive home, exhausted, around one in the morning, and be back at the farm eight hours later. Somehow, I found the time to field the hundreds of emails we received each week and lead tours for curious visitors. Our days were fourteen, fifteen, sixteen hours long, six, sometimes seven days a week. It was an unsustainable amount of work that would have burned us out in time. But even putting in that many hours wasn't enough. We needed help.

And help we would receive! We are incredibly fortunate here in New York to be one of just a few farms in a city full of smart, ambitious individuals who want to learn about agriculture. The first of these folks to approach us was Rob Lateiner.

He emailed us in February 2010, three months before we laid down the soil on our flagship farm, and said he had been working at a farm called Glynwood, in Cold Spring, New York, and now was thinking of starting his own rooftop farm but wasn't ready to "put down roots." He'd seen early murmurings of our project in the press and wanted in. We loved that he had some experience farming (and the roots pun didn't hurt, either). That first season, Rob was at the farm as often as, if not more than, Gwen or me. He and Ben were attached at the hip, and you could see just how invested he was in the farm by how deeply his brow would furrow when he looked out at a bed germinating poorly. Over time, he literally invested in the farm and is now a partial owner of the business. As the first season wound down, he decided to strike out on his own, moving to the West Coast to study viticulture, but he remains a dear friend and partner, and visits us annually to catch up.

Two months after Rob's email came in, we received another fortuitous message, this time from Hester Griffin, a sophomore environmental studies major at the New School, who was focusing on urban ecosystems and sustainable design. Just to ice the cake, Hester's own entrepreneurialism led her to seek out grant funding from her school for her time with us, which she secured for not only the first season but our second as well, when she went on to head up our small but growing band of trainees as team leader. She has since studied with Eliot Coleman at Four Seasons Farm in Maine, and now works at Queens County Farm Museum and visits regularly (though not as often as we wish she would!).

Rob and Hester were essential in helping us run the farm, especially that first season. But the day-to-day operations are only part of running a small business. When we'd launched, and Chris and Brandon had gone back to running Roberta's, we found ourselves with two fewer voices weighing in on big-picture decisions. And with our business modeled on an aggressive expansion plan, we needed to be focused on the big picture. Zooming out wasn't easy with the operational minutiae of our brand-new and very needy business demanding every ounce of our time and attention. Asking a first-year business operator to think about her next big move is like asking the sleep-deprived parent of a newborn baby when she plans on having her next kid.

Which is why we all knew it was kismet when we met Chase.

Our first acquisition to the management team came about a year after we opened, in the form of about 150,000 buzzing insects. Fortunately, these insects were attached to a man in a beekeeper's suit with over two decades of business experience and the energy level of a high school senior on his last day of class. His name was Chase Emmons.

Like me, Chase is a city kid, and the two of us often laugh about our childhoods spent terrified of bees. But sometimes life takes us down unexpected paths. Chase, who is a bit older than the rest of us, began his journey into urban agriculture through a circuitous route. He and his father were early franchisers of The Princeton Review, the test prep company, and jumped at the opportunity to franchise the lucrative Western Massachusetts chapter, in the heart of boarding school territory. Running a business in Western Massachusetts, however, required that they be in that area at least part-time, so they bought a house nestled in an orchard near Amherst. Then one day a friend who lived nearby called and said "Dude, I got a beehive!" Chase did not share his enthusiasm. "Are you fucking insane?" he asked. But his friend persisted, swearing that Chase would be as enamored with the bees as he had been and eventually talked him into coming to see the hive.

In spite of himself, Chase was indeed amazed by the industrious creatures, oblivious to their human keeper, diligently making their way in and out of the hive. And of course, he had just acquired an orchard, which needed a healthy population of pollinators to flourish. Within a year, Chase found himself a mentor, adopted a few hives of his own, and was enjoying the increased productivity of his apple trees thanks to his new farmhands.

Meanwhile, those back in his native New York City were still living under the yoke of Mayor Giuliani, who, in 1999, added honeybees to the list of "dangerous animals" that were banned within city limits. The list included pit vipers, crocodiles, and lions, and carried a $2,000 fine for anyone found with the offending creatures. A few advocates and seasoned beekeepers put in some serious work on getting the ban lifted, and after eleven years, in spring 2010, the city changed the law, and beekeepers of the five boroughs were finally able to come out from behind their veils!

When Chase heard that he might be able to bring his newfound passion back to his hometown, he was immediately excited. And when Chase gets excited, he gets *really* excited. He wasn't just thinking about having a hive or two in the backyard of his family's West Village home; nah, that would be child's play. Chase is a serial entrepreneur, and he saw an opportunity to start a business. He started doing market research and found there was a huge demand for local honey. There were, at the time, very few vendors selling local NYC honey, and one of the most popular, Andrew's Honey, helmed by Andrew Coté, one of the advocates responsible for getting beekeeping legalized, regularly sold out at the Union Square Greenmarket. Over coffees with Andrew and as many other veteran beeks as Chase could get to lend him half an hour of their time, he was assured that urban beekeeping was safe and that the honey was delicious and clean. He crunched some numbers and found that a modest capital investment would provide a pretty decent re-

turn, and he grew more and more convinced that an urban apiary was a viable model.

When he came across early press on Brooklyn Grange in
late 2009, Chase immediately saw synergy between his urban
apiary concept and our nascent farming business. A few months
later, Chase was introduced to us via email through an old high
school friend now working in urban agriculture. He wasted no
time in asking Ben if he could come up for a visit, seeing an
opportunity to pitch us his urban apiary concept.

Once he did, he found himself digging the scrappy, do-it-
yourself vibe of the farm, and was impressed by the fact that
we'd pulled off something of this scale. Chase had grown up
playing on the abandoned High Line rail tracks of Manhattan's
West Side, and like any good city kid, he had a penchant for
secret, elevated spaces that felt illicit and antiestablishment. The
farm was right up his alley. Plus, Chase prides himself on his
shrewd New Yorker instincts. His finely tuned business radar
said that we were a smart bet, and he saw the value that each of
us brought to the table. While most early visitors were congrat-
ulating us on getting the farm built, Chase was already thinking of what we could do next.

Thus began Chase's period of "lurking," as he calls it. He
spent that first day hanging around the farm, checking out our
operations, and asking as many questions as he could. A few
weeks later, he came to a dinner on the roof. It was a beauti-

ful night: the roof was lit by lanterns and dinner was served on boards plunked down atop some decommissioned steel girders that were, until that evening, wasted space. We'd hauled up palettes and boards to use as decking around the awkwardly tall platform, and borrowed office chairs from a fellow tenant downstairs. Chase happened to be seated next to a neighborhood guy named Lou, who used to come by and drive Ben around on deliveries for fun. Lou regaled Chase with tales from that first season of farming: hauling veggies around in Ben's biodiesel Mercedes sedan with the cranky tank; getting into traffic jams and throwing radishes at offending trucks blocking the box; bungee cording the trunk down around triple stacks of packed crates; and bottoming out on the potholed roads during tomato season deliveries, when the car was back-loaded so bad the tail pipe was practically dragging on the ground.

At this point, between the DIY underground feel and the ridiculous cast of characters, Chase was smitten, and he wanted in. The feeling was entirely mutual. We were impressed by how determined Chase was to create a business out of legalized beekeeping. He clearly sensed that the recent change in legislation would mean a big uptick of interest in the practice, and he saw an opportunity to not only create revenue but contribute to the community building around the honeybees of New York City. Like us, he recognized a cultural movement happening and a way to engage with it commercially. He had done his due diligence. He had run numbers. He was approaching it from a practical, fiscal perspective, as well as a social one. He was a kindred entrepreneurial spirit.

As luck would have it, we had a share of equity to spare that we had held in reserve in case we found ourselves short on cash, so we struck a deal. First off, Chase said, we had to handle this vehicle situation. A fussy biodiesel sedan with broken A/C was not an adequate delivery method. He had a Dodge Caravan he was going to sell anyway, so we looked up the Blue Book value—at the time, $2,000—and factored that into the deal. Then he made the case for more bees. We had one hive at the time, managed by our friend Stephanos, which was sufficient in pollinating our fields, but Chase maintained that we were missing an opportunity to add honey to our product lineup, and that with a few additional hives, we could be swimming in liquid gold. Ben looked over the basic capital costs and projected honey revenue, and was impressed by some promising figures. So after a few calculations, we arrived at a market-value deal: we traded him our remaining share of equity in exchange for four beehives, a van, and a little bit of cash.

It was a low-commitment deal. We waded into the relationship, and the apiary project, instead of diving in. Ben, Gwen, and I were protective of our nascent business, and we weren't prepared to welcome a newcomer without fully vetting him. And for his part, while Chase has a great deal of enthusiasm, he knew better than to cannonball into a deal that could drown him in responsibility. But in the year that followed, as the opportunity to open a second location at the Brooklyn Navy Yard became more and more real, and a second round of financing came with it, we found that Chase was exactly the man we needed to shore up the craft. He loved teaching our team about beekeeping, and we loved learning. But more than anything, he created a balance and objectivity in the group and brought a fresh set of eyes to everything we did.

Chase is also in his forties, and while he's arguably more youthful (certainly physically fitter and better versed in pop culture and social media) than the rest of us, we were still in our late twenties at that point. A bit of help convincing stuffy suits of our credibility couldn't hurt. Plus, it can be hard to see your own achievements from the inside, and even harder to think about replicating them when achieving them took everything out of you in the first place. But as a newcomer who hadn't witnessed the blood, sweat, and tears we'd poured into raising funds for, seeking out, and installing the flagship farm, Chase only saw the products of our efforts, not the toll they had taken on us. So not only did he have a tremendous amount of faith that we could expand our business, he also had no compunction crowing about our achievements to anyone and everyone he thought could help us meet our goals of farming additional roofs in New York City.

While some might assume that, given his experience, Chase would be the voice of reason among us, he's often the grandest thinker in our internal meetings. After a year of working hard to get through the day-to-day, we'd grown slightly less bold than we'd been when we were dreaming up the project. The reality of operating our business had made us wary of taking on more and spreading ourselves even thinner. So despite the fact that we tease him for the refrain that's become something of a catchphrase, his constant exhortations of "Hear me out, I've got a crazy idea!" have, on more than one occasion, led to some of our favorite projects and enterprises.

Just as Chase's bees each have a role to play in the health of the hive, so, too, does every member of our farmily play a crucial role in the health of our business. Our roles are less hierarchical, but just as a hive's worker bees shift positions, we've all fulfilled different functions over the years as our farm and our team have matured. Just as a strong queen would be nothing without her colony, and just as the nectar brought home by foragers would never be converted to honey without the hard work of the fanning caste, we all need one another.

As operators, we are a pretty wildly diverse group. More than our different competencies, it's our complementary dispositions that suited us to running our business well. Gwen, for example, is incredibly capable, and extremely efficient. She turned our shipping container into a walk-in refrigerator in under a week, and puts grant applications together in a matter of hours. She built most of our physical infrastructure on the farm, as well as our Web site, a skill that she taught herself. But more than her handiness, it's her attitude that helps our business thrive. She believes in getting things done. She is fearless.

I couldn't be more different. I'm the very definition of a disaster forecaster: I hem and I haw. I like to walk through every possible hypothetical scenario of how a project will go down, think through the most infinitesimal details, and create contingency plans for our contingency plans. I believe in making things as perfect as they can be before we put a plan into action, and that often means I need time to reflect on a project before I feel like we're ready to dive in. But that can really slow us down, and working too slowly can cripple a small business. If it weren't for the brisk pace Gwen sets, I might be paralyzed by my obsessive exactitude. Yet without my attention to detail, she might miss an opportunity or have to resolve a challenge on the fly that could have been headed off at the pass with a carefully devised plan of action.

Chase and I are a lot alike—perhaps by virtue of the fact that we're both high-energy New Yorkers—except that instead of seeing potential for disaster, he sees potential for success. His confidence in the virtues of our team and our business crumbles even my trepidation. Often, he'll come up with one of his "crazy ideas," and where I see trouble, he sees endless opportunities. I'll throw out a bunch of reasons that it's impractical and list all the things that could go wrong; he'll counter with reasons we should take the chance and all the doors it could open; we'll hash out the logistics for a bit, and then come to consensus before we bring the idea to fruition, or at least to the rest of the group. We probably argue more than any other two members of the team, but it's always productive. At the end of the day, despite our fierce debates, we work together incredibly well, not only because my fastidiousness and his enthusiasm create a balance, but because we trust, respect, and admire each other. When push comes to shove, we've got each other's backs, and we know it.

And then there's Ben.

It's hard to describe the role Ben plays on our team, but maybe the best way of putting it is that he sees the forest for the trees. While Chase is excitedly pitching the forest to a potential partner as a magical place worthy of their investment, I'm turning over every last leaf on the forest floor to inspect for pests and diseases, and Gwen's already gone to the nursery and bought a bunch of saplings, which she's busy transplanting like some superhuman Johnny Appleseed. But Ben . . . Ben is looking at the big picture. He's projecting what the forest will look like five and ten years from now. He's looking at how the forest will interact with our adjacent fields.

Ben does everything. He does the physical work and the cerebral. He engineers the farms, and then he gets out there and executes the systems he's designed. He makes everyone feel like they have a place, somehow, even when he doesn't remember names. He leads by example; there is no one more hardworking. And in spite of everything he does, Ben always finds the time to do the single most important thing a leader can do: he listens. It's a hard skill to quantify, but an essential one for a small business as firmly rooted in the community as ours is. He's out at events and talks all the time, keeping a finger on the pulse no matter how full his hands are. He accepts more invitations than a reasonable person should, and sleeps less than we'd like. He hears our team, what they want to do, how they want to grow themselves and the business, and he advocates for everyone. That is what truly makes him a great leader: not that his word rules, or that people fear letting him down. Rather, everyone on our team knows they are being heard.

In addition to being a good listener, Ben is also incredibly—almost pathologically—positive. He doesn't get pessimistic, he isn't easily frustrated, and he's quick to laugh. We all left jobs we didn't love to start the farm, and that really helps to remind us that we do what we do because we love it, because it's fun. But Ben's cheer also helps to set the tone. So in all but the most stressful situations—and there have certainly been a few of those over the years—we've kept it fun. In those early days, when we were working ourselves to the bone, the farm still felt like somewhere you wanted to be. We would listen and sing along to Creedence Clearwater Revival while we sorted tomatoes, and make bad dad jokes while sweating it out over a harvest on a hot day. We'd sneak a round of beers at the end of a successful farm stand. The positive atmosphere we cultivated allowed us to see challenges as exciting possibilities, and failures as something from which we could grow.

Ben's positivity is at the center of our company culture. It's a tough word to define, but to anyone who spends as much time at work as we do, it's an important one. Company culture isn't about pizza parties or summer Fridays. It's not about fair and equitable HR practices like paid maternity leave, or even about a company's mission—though an organization that offers benefits and values its employees' contributions will certainly be more successful in achieving theirs. Rather, it's an attitude of an organization—its personality. Though we all worked together to create our company culture, and brought our own individual personalities to bear shaping the character of our organization, Ben's positivity was without a doubt the overwhelming drive behind Brooklyn Grange's organizational climate. His default disposition is upbeat. He almost never uses the word "hate." He says hello to everyone, whether it's a future bride and groom on a site visit with our events team, or an elevator repairman climbing up a bulkhead to check an electrical connection.

Being around someone that cheerful, helpful, and friendly is infectious, and it spread to each of our departments. I made it our communications policy to reply to each and every email, even if it's a message asking for something we don't sell, like young tomato plants. Instead of blowing off the inquiry because there's nothing in it for us, or responding with a negative "No, sorry," we send a note with recommendations on where to get the best tomato seedlings in town. It's the neighborly thing to do, and the sweet notes of gratitude we get in response fuel us for sending the next email.

While thank-you notes bolster our energy, and a positive atmosphere puts a spring in our step, cheer is no substitute for sleep. We learned quickly in the first year of operating the farm that passion and a positive attitude can't replace rest, and we realized that we were working ourselves too hard. Ben wasn't sleeping; you could tell just by glancing at him. Perhaps it was the pressure of being the only paid member, but Gwen and I had to beg him to start taking one day off each week. I took over our Saturday farm stand, and Gwen started leading the Saturday open house at the flagship farm. As we were pulling into the market on Ben's very first free Saturday, I checked my email. It was nine a.m. and Ben had already sent an email with three spreadsheets charting revenue growth. That's not a day off! But Ben believes that he has an obligation to our business, and our staff, to work as much as it takes to keep Brooklyn Grange moving forward. Moreover, he loves what he does, and it's immediately apparent. That kind of work ethic—never feigned, totally genuine—is what inspires our team to strive. It's what makes us all want to be the best professionals that we can be.

By the time we closed out the 2011 season, we were wiped out. While Chase still had some sweat equity due, having just joined the business a year earlier, Gwen and I needed to start getting paid. Not only were we working way too hard not to be compensated, but we knew Ben would never take any time off unless he ceased to feel the weight of his salary differentiating his time from ours. Fortunately, we had locked in a lease at the Brooklyn Navy Yard and would be installing a second farm, more than doubling our production, the following spring. Still, that didn't guarantee we would have enough money coming in to support us all. We knew we would have to create the revenue or we wouldn't be able to make ends meet. Our salaries weren't guaranteed; they were contingent on our success. If it weren't for what happened next, we might not have made the leap and started paying ourselves. We might have held on to our off-farm jobs till we saw how the upcoming seasons shook out financially.

Sometimes, though, life makes decisions for you. By the end of our second season, Gwen had an infant son to look after, and I had two herniated discs in my lower spine from spending sixteen hours a day lugging bottles upstairs to stock the bar and hauling compost up to the farm. Neither of us was able to maintain two jobs anymore. We knew our workload was unsustainable; we had always intended to get the business to a point where we were working more reasonable hours for which we were fairly compensated, but ultimately, it was circumstance that determined when we made the transition.

So we set out to create the revenue we needed to support

ourselves, which meant taking some of Ben's overwhelming load of job responsibilities and improving on them, as well as creating new revenue streams. It's important to note here that we didn't take it for granted that Gwen and I were a natural fit as operators. Sometimes the founders of a business aren't the right people to run it. Sometimes, as the business matures, it grows apart from its founders and requires an outsider with a skill set better matched to its needs at that point in its development. If Chris hadn't known himself as well as he did, for example, and had tried to stick it out as a farm operator instead of focusing on expanding his restaurant business, he would have found himself both bored by the repetitive, detail-focused work and annoyed by the constant stream of enthusiastic people coming up for visits.

This was not the case with Gwen or me. There were parts of Ben's job with which we'd already been helping, and it was a natural transition for us to shoulder a greater share of those responsibilities. For example, Gwen had grown up gardening and had a year of professional farming under her belt, so she had always been capable of running the show at the farm when Ben was out on a delivery or in a meeting. Additionally, her efficiency and handiness made her a capable farm manager: she got the seeds in on schedule and the weeds out before we knew what hit us, all without skipping a beat when it came to her accounting duties. So she was a natural fit to become farm manager of the flagship farm in 2012 when Ben needed to focus on the Navy Yard.

Meanwhile, my years working in the restaurant industry meant that I was experienced in two areas that needed help: dealing with chefs and hospitality. Ben was running sales at the time, and with everything else he had going on—which was, well, everything—he was barely managing to keep up. He sold everything we grew, but without a spare second to sit down and create efficient systems for doing so, he was hemorrhaging time bringing tiny thirty-dollar orders across town. I had already been handling the orders I brought to the restaurant where I'd been bartending and had a good sense of the job to begin with. So Ben and I strategized a standing-order system through which chefs would commit to taking a certain amount of salad greens—our most profitable crop—each week, thus informing us of exactly how much we needed to plant, and saving the time of piecing together buyers to take our harvest from day to day. We also started enforcing delivery minimums, which often meant being a bit tough with the very folks who had supported us from day one. These may seem like obvious policies to put in place, and it's not as though Ben had never considered enrolling accounts in standing orders or enforcing minimums before I took over sales, but he's incredibly loyal and kind of a pushover, so saying no to chefs, especially those who were early supporters and were patient through our growing pains, can be tough for him. I have no problem with it whatsoever.

Revenues from vegetable sales increased dramatically the year I took over. We can attribute this partly to the fact that I had a bit more time to run a tighter ship and that I was excited about taking on a new challenge. But a larger cause of the increase was that my undivided attention to the business gave Ben the latitude to focus on growing more efficiently, which meant he could produce more vegetables for me to sell. Putting me on salary—investing in me, as it were—earned us not just a director of sales and a more effective director of events and director of communications and public relations (yes, I had three titles; we've since trimmed it down to vice president) but also a more focused and successful head farmer.

We found our roles. We figured out what we were good at and, just as important, how those skills could contribute to the bottom line. And we respected one another's autonomy over our respective domains. When I started booking events, we were mostly hosting our restaurant friends for ticketed parties for which the general public would pay maybe fifty, sixty bucks to attend. Seeing the potential, Ben and Gwen were quick to ask how they could help me increase business, and when I said better facilities—starting with an actual dinner table on which guests could dine—they wasted no time in enlisting an architect friend to help design and build one.

I knew I had their support. But things got a bit more complicated when I began booking private events. Instead of plunking down less than they'd spend on a few rounds of drinks to come up for an evening, private events clients were now willing to spend thousands of dollars on a caterer and to rent out our space, an arrangement that put a lot more pressure on me than the ticketed dinners.

Early on, a client approached us about booking the farm for an elaborate dinner. It was going to be complicated, and they clearly expected it to be executed flawlessly. I wasn't sure we could pull it off—at that time, we had zero infrastructure besides our new table and some wonky benches—but I was willing to give it a shot. I knew it would take a lot of my time to produce, and be a bit of a strain on the farm to boot, so I adjusted my quote accordingly. The client balked at the price (which in retrospect, is laughable—I think I asked them for $750, which for a private rooftop venue in New York City is unheard of) and asked a friend they and Ben shared to reach out to Ben and ask him to come down in price.

The conversation that ensued between Ben and me was intense. He was adamant that I needed to take more chances and book more business, even if it meant charging less. His point was a fair one: we'd never gain traction as an events space if we didn't do some events. After all, every event we hosted was an advertisement of our space to those who attended it. I countered that it wouldn't be a very good advertisement if we fell flat on our face. I foresaw inconsistency between what the guest expected and what we could provide for the amount of money they wanted to pay, and I let him know just how much pressure it was to have that expectation falling on my shoulders, and my shoulders alone.

Because we had created a culture of mutual respect for each other, and trust each other to run our departments, Ben relented. He ended up telling me that he saw my point, and that he would stand behind whatever decision I thought was best. Instead of feeling like the expectation was on me alone, I was bolstered by having him in my corner. With his support, and the understanding that I was taking a bit of a leap, I came down just slightly in price and booked the gig. It was a shitshow but an important learning experience for me. And when we ended up blowing a fuse an hour before the event was set to begin, losing our power on the roof, I didn't hesitate to call Ben, who dropped what he was doing, drove to Home Depot, rented a generator, and made it back to the farm before the guests noticed anything was wrong. The rest of the event went well enough, and the client was happy. Neither of us ever said, "I told you so." We were both right, and better yet, we had heard each other. Moreover, we were able to have a productive off-season conversation about what resources the events program needed for me to be able to host with less hassle.

The early development of our events department is just one example of our culture of trust and mutual respect. When Ben, Gwen, and Chase push me to take chances and move quickly,

I don't take it as an insult or a judgment that I'm working too slowly; rather, I give them the benefit of the doubt and take it as a vote of confidence. They know I'm capable and thorough but also very self-critical. So when they push, rather than hearing a criticism, I hear them telling me that my "OK" is most people's "excellent." And the converse is true as well. When one of them thinks they might be moving too quickly on something, or wants a sounding board before making a decision, they might ask me to help them assess the potential risks. If they want to feel better about saying no to someone, I'm their first call. We balance one another out that way.

But my perfectionism and self-critical nature make me a bit of a Nervous Nancy, and I show it all over my face. So when we started booking weddings, it quickly became clear that I was not good at them. It's the most important day of a couple's life, and that's just too much pressure for someone as tightly wound as I am. I am great at planning the thing, handling all the logistics, but when it comes to client relationships, I would only stress the bride and groom out. And forget about running the show on the big day itself! I wasn't happy, and I could tell the clients were picking up on my anxiety. Because I knew my partners had faith in me, I wasn't afraid that owning up to my shortcoming would cause them to devalue me as a team member. I was able to admit that I needed help.

Fortunately for us all, I had received a call a few weeks prior from a recent college graduate, the daughter of a former colleague, by the name of Michele Kaufman, asking if she could shadow me in the office and learn more about the business. I had immediately agreed, desperate for help with communications and PR, events, and sales.

I quickly realized something that isn't always the easiest thing to accept: Michele was better at my job than I was. Don't get me wrong, she was a kid. She was so green when she started out that she was practically glowing. But she's also smart as a whip and has impeccable instincts. She's affable and disarming, and reads people like a picture book. I recognized that there was one thing and one thing only that stood between us (besides my transparent anxiety that was driving potential wedding clients away), and that was confidence. She simply needed to learn the ropes and gain some notches in her belt before she could be assured that she was as capable as I was. Which she did, and quickly.

More than anything, though, Michele is superpositive and has a tremendous amount of equanimity. I've watched her soldier through situations that make me want to throw up, all with a smile on her face. As important as the fact that she was calm with our events clients was the fact that Ben, Gwen, and Chase absolutely loved her. She was pleasant and lighthearted. She never complained and was quick to get excited about a new chicken joining the flock or a crop we were trying to grow for the first time. She loved the farm, and it showed.

Michele is truly an example of hiring someone based on personality over skill set, and it was a gamble we've never regretted for a second. That being said, we're cautious, especially when it comes to finances. We really don't like to commit to spending money we don't already have in the bank. So when we replaced me with Michele as our director of events, we made her position commission based: as much as we loved her, we did have a bottom line to consider, and she was inexperienced. Once she exceeded expectations in her first season on the job, we offered to transition her to salary for her second season, at a significant pay increase over the commission she'd made the year before. But wouldn't you know, Michele *requested* to remain on commission. It challenged her, she said, and she liked competing with her previous record. It helped her form clear goals and be a bit sharkier. We were floored.

Michele isn't the only member of our team who is a walking, talking argument for hiring based on compatibility with company culture. When we hired Bradley Fleming as the farm manager of our flagship farm to replace Gwen and free her up for another project, we chose him over other applicants mostly because he was always showing up to things: farming talks, potluck events . . . he was everywhere! He got the job because he was more interested in and enthusiastic about it than the other candidates, such as the more experienced applicant who lived down the street but had never even visited the farm. Bradley, on the contrary, is passionate about the social dimension of Brooklyn Grange, and the food system in general, and that passion is infectious. And we try to grow our business into our team as much as we grow our team into our business. Bradley came from a CSA farm, where he had hundreds of members to feed. He loves his CSA members more than any other dimension of the job, so in part because of his keenness for the program, we increased the size of our CSA at the flagship farm.

The farm manager we hired to replace Ben at the Navy Yard, Matt Jefferson, is one tough cookie. He's fast as shit, superproductive, and loves a challenge. Matt is constantly pushing himself and the farm he manages, so he's great at filling aggressive wholesale orders. When I was still doing sales, I'd often commit more than we had to our accounts: he'd say we had eighty-five pounds of greens available, and I'd sell a hundred. He'd always reply to my apologetic emails letting him know I could dial back each order by a pound or two with a guffaw: "A hundred pounds, huh? It's gonna be tight, but we can do it." To that end, we've funneled most of our wholesale business to the Navy Yard farm. When he increased productivity to the degree that we could afford to hire him a helping hand, we didn't put a job ad out searching for an experienced farmer. Rather, we hired Alia, the career-changing former lawyer who had begun hanging around every day trying to learn as much about farming as possible. We hired her in large part because Matt loved working with her. It didn't hurt that she could prep a bed to be planted faster than anyone had ever seen.

Bradley's right-hand woman, whom we call Cashew (to differentiate her from Michele Kaufman) had great professional chemistry with Bradley, and Robyn, our events manager, clicked with Michele Kaufman right away. Our team basically formed itself. Sure, our hires are all smart, capable, and trustworthy folks, and that helps a lot, but more than being highly skilled, it's about being highly compatible. Especially on those days when it's pissing rain and freezing cold and you have a huge pick list, it doesn't matter how much your colleague knows about soil science, it matters that she shows up on time, is ready to work hard, and can make you laugh while you're at it.

Our chief financial officer, Melissa Kuzoian, is the glue that holds it all together. At twenty-four, she may seem young to have earned the title of CFO, but she truly has grown beyond the office manager we hired her to be and into a shrewd analyst and a trusted advisor. But her CFO title could easily stand in for another of her crucial roles: chief friendship officer. Melissa plans all of our farmily outings. She gets us all tickets to see our local minor-league baseball team, the Brooklyn Cyclones, including everyone's significant others and kids. She organizes team dinners, makes fresh cookies for meetings, and has become the master of vegan, gluten-free baking, since Bradley doesn't eat animal products or wheat. She makes everyone feel not just a part of the team but a part of the farmily.

It's not hard. At the farm, everyone gets to know one another, and fast. There are too many tasks that require two sets of hands to go it alone. You need help to move a heavy thing or a second opinion on how to solve a problem. And it transcends the work. When I had to move out of my apartment unexpectedly, at a particularly busy time of year, our entire team reached out independently of one another to offer their help. Bradley said he could drive my things over to my new place in the farm van; everyone came over one night and ate Thai takeout and painted. I was surrounded by support not just at work, but even once we clocked out.

The staff of Brooklyn Grange are all friends at this point. They didn't know one another when they started working at the farm, but they spend their time off together because they rarely tire of one another's companionship. They've vacationed together. They're pals. It happens when you work across a row from someone, sweat it out with someone, problem solve with someone, work late nights followed by early mornings with someone. When one farm manager has a monster harvest and a light team, and the other shows up to pinch-hit on the fly, you can't help but feel warmth and gratitude toward your colleague. We buy one another coffees often and know how everyone takes their cup (except forgetful Ben, of whose signature move we've learned to be wary: unsure of whether someone takes sugar, he'll put one or two in the bottom of the cup and simply refrain from stirring it. Good—until the last drop . . .).

Let us make one thing clear, though: Ben, Gwen, Chase, and I, the owners of the business, are not friends. We love and respect one another, and in a lot of ways, we're closer than friends, or even family. Occasionally, Chase and I even yell at each other—actually raise our voices and shout—like brother and sister. It's how we communicate sometimes because we are both passionate, loud New Yorkers, and we know that when we're hollering, as Chase would put it, "It's about the problem, not the person."

The methods we've found of communicating as business partners and the professional relationships we've forged have been possible *because* we were not friends to begin with. We went into business together not because we wanted to work with our pals, but because we saw in one another the best partners for the job. Which is important, because the person sitting across from you at the conference table *isn't* a pal; it creates cognitive dissonance if you're looking at your friend but hearing them tell you the margins on your department are weak. We know one another as professional people first and foremost rather than social animals. When one of us is late to a morning meeting, there's no personal context projected on it: it's not "Were you out at the bar too late last night?" Instead, it's "Please don't be late again; we all need to be respectful of one another's time." In a way, it has allowed us to grow into the professional selves we strive to be, without the preconceived expectations we might have of childhood pals overshadowing our achievements.

It also helps, when you work as much as we do, to be able to step away from it all when you do get time off. I love my partners dearly, but frankly, when I've put in seventy hours over six straight days, the last thing I want to do on my one day off is see any of their faces. Our brains need a rest from interacting with one another. And we form certain associations with people. If we had to switch gears from being professionally supportive to being emotionally supportive on a regular basis, it would be confusing, if not exhausting. Of course from time to time we perform double duties: the breakups, the sick relatives . . . we've certainly been friends and confidants for one another over the years. We all made the trip to Maine when Gwen and Christopher tied the knot, and there wasn't a dry eye among us. But at the end of the day, we are business partners, and that is a kind of respectful support that, when all else in your life is uncertain, when your relationships are chaotic and your personal life is a mess, can be more of a comfort and a source of equanimity than anything else. We can't cure a cousin of cancer or mend a failing relationship, but we can do right by our business, and we know we'll have three people who appreciate and respect us for it.

We've watched so many of our colleagues' businesses fall apart because of infighting, yet we've managed to get through some pretty major disagreements because our relationships are predicated on one shared motivation: to succeed as an organization. We give one another the benefit of the doubt that the business is our first priority, so when we disagree, we don't take it personally. In fact, the more passionate our arguments are, the more we respect one another's fierce dedication to the work we are doing.

Sure, money still causes tensions, especially because we often don't have enough of it or work too much for too little of it. But as owners of the business, Brooklyn Grange's success is our shared profit. We can only imagine that the situation would be a bit different if we had an excess of money: typically, when a business starts realizing seven-figure profits, things take a different tone. Maybe we'll be lucky enough to face that problem someday. We're becoming more and more profitable as each season passes. A big part of that success is seeking out new ventures and becoming better at striking deals. And when we walk into meetings with smooth-talking executives with business degrees and corner offices, we know we've got an edge on them: We've got our team. We've got one another.

7

GROWING ORGANICALLY

Knowing When to Sign a Deal

At Brooklyn Grange, we sometimes wonder what first impressions people have of us as a group. We've walked into business meetings in dirt-smeared jeans; Gwen's shown up with a baby strapped to her back; I almost always have my bike helmet and am chugging from a dinged-up metal water bottle; Chase wears running gear everywhere he goes (in case, we assume, he is challenged to a spontaneous race). Ben once arrived to a site visit of an iconic New York City building, where we were meeting the senior vice president of the most prominent commercial real estate firm in town, carrying one lonesome mud-caked boot. But if the suits we've met with over the years had any doubts about our seriousness based on our appearance, we've more often than not made short work of their expectations.

In our first five years of operating, we looked at dozens of potential locations and met with as many slick-talking real estate players, but at the time of this writing, though we are in negotiations with a landlord about leasing a third roof, we only have two farms. Our original business plan projected us farming *seven* roofs by now. Yet we don't consider that a failure; on the contrary, we've learned a lot about making deals since we launched our business, and we now understand that we would have been fools to take on that much real estate that quickly.

So instead of walking into site visits and initial meetings with the attitude that we need to strike a deal in order to reach a goal we set for ourselves before we'd launched our business, we tend to be cautious yet decisive with potential new partners. We might dream big, but when it comes to making deals, we're firmly grounded in reality.

Chase likes to remind us that the number one reason small businesses fail is that they expand too quickly. That's important to remember, because it can be tempting to get excited about the inquiries that come rolling in during the first couple years of success and visibility. A few magazine articles come out, a spot airs on NPR, and suddenly you're fielding calls from property owners up and down the Eastern Seaboard. It's validating, and after slogging through the start-up phase, it feels good to be pursued. You think, "A Manhattan roof would take us to the next level," or maybe "I wouldn't mind moving to Philly to start an outpost of our organization there!" And when you get further into conversations, you remember that you'd essentially be replicating the start-up slog all over again, except this time, you'd have to maintain day-to-day operations at your existing sites simultaneously.

When opportunity knocks, we always open the door and see who's calling before we invite anyone inside. While exploring an opportunity is relatively harmless, once a deal is signed, you've got to live with it. To that end, we've walked away from some prospects that seemed at first glance to be dreams come true.

One such option presented itself a few seasons back when the landlords of our flagship farm, Acumen Capital Partners, bought the former Pfizer pharmaceutical manufacturing plant in Brooklyn. It's a massive property and was built to accommodate superheavy machinery, so we were fairly certain we'd have no issues with the weight rating. Plus, we were already in bed with Acumen at the flagship farm, and the devil you know is always better than the one you don't. We were loyal to them, and we believed them to be loyal to us. So when they approached us about farming their roof, we tried every which way to figure out how to make it work. But with a billion different levels jutting out here and there, and mechanicals taking up well over half the space, it simply wasn't feasible. When we told them we were passing, they were quick to let us know that they'd found another farmer who was happy to apply for the DEP green roof grant, and they would simply proceed in negotiating a deal with her. When the DEP announced their grantees for that year, and she was among them, a glimmer of doubt ran through us: Had we made a mistake? What did she see in the roof that we had missed? How did she plan to make it work?

Well, that was three years ago, and that grant money was left sitting on the table, most likely because the farmer they'd found to occupy the space realized what we knew at first glance: it just wasn't a good fit for a farm. It felt good to know we had made the right choice, but it also reminded us that Acumen was running a business of its own. Of course we had always known that, but as you get better acquainted with your company's partners, especially when you work together well and seem to want the same things, it's worth reminding yourself that they, too, have a bottom line. If they are smart operators, they will be motivated by self-interest, and if push comes to shove, they will not hesitate to do what's best for them.

All told, though, we're lucky to work with Acumen. We've met some real stinkers in the developer world over the years, and we've learned how to distinguish between shrewd business-people and the straight-up assholes who would sell their own mothers up the river for a dime. Far more difficult to assess are the huge development firms, with so many different players at bat that just when you get to know one of them, some new joker shows up swinging. We experienced this scenario for the first time not long ago, when we were approached to put a farm on the roof of a new luxury development on the Lower East Side. Gwen spent hours in meetings with the developers, drawing up proposals that were less focused on revenue charts, as our early business plans were, and instead filled with beautiful mock-ups of a well-maintained mini farm, with a space for yoga classes and events, and a compost operation tucked away from any tenants' windows. We all spent time in meetings with the developers, who had various concerns about whether the limousine-liberal buyers they hoped to attract would be willing to overlook sweaty farmers, smelly compost, and the clinking of glasses after dark in the service of having a farm on their roof.

We were patient, but by the time we'd been passed off to the third set of folks working on the project, we realized who we were dealing with. The teams who shepherded the development through its successive stages were cogs in a machine. Every time we spoke to a new team coming aboard the project, we had to start from the top. And with every meeting, the area they had allotted to the farm seemed to shrink! When they expressed reservations about events for the fifteenth time, while shaving off more and more square feet from the event space, we realized they hadn't been listening to us at all. They didn't know—or care—what was required for us to succeed as a rooftop farming business. At first we had thought it might be an opportunity to break into a new world; Chase had argued that it didn't matter if we built it or not, we should just get our name attached to the project so other developers realized our value.

But the developer was so far off base and the project changed hands so many times that it turned out to be a massive time suck for us. Even if we'd been desperate and had all the time in the world, working with a machine as large and impersonal as that particular firm was a dangerous game. They were so singularly focused on profit and uninterested in anything beyond running numbers that they simply weren't a good fit for a business as complex, nuanced, and community focused as ours. Also, because they were such a huge operation, and as a consequence communicated among themselves so inefficiently, we realized no project we could ever build with them would reflect well on us.

On other occasions, we've walked into conversations thinking they wouldn't end well, only to be pleasantly surprised. As the head of our design and installations department, Gwen tends to be more mindful of expansion opportunities than any other member of our team, and she's often the first responder when we receive an inquiry from a building owner. With her can-do attitude and flexibility, she's the perfect woman for the job. She never walks onto a roof or terrace, or into a backyard or vacant lot, and tries to impose our vision of a farm upon the space; rather, she looks at the space and tries to imagine what's possible there.

If a space is too small for us to lease and farm commercially, but the landlord is dead set on having a green roof, Gwen might suggest native wildflowers and plants that are beneficial to pollinators instead. If she can write a proposal and receive grant funding to build the green space, she has an even better chance of scoring us a job. While an installation job—even with a maintenance contract attached—isn't quite as exciting as a third location for Brooklyn Grange, it's solid revenue, and an important part of our business. It's a testament to Gwen's open-mindedness that she has done a laudable job of making hay when the sun ostensibly isn't shining (and has even built herb gardens where the sun literally isn't shining at all).

The principle of letting a space speak to you is an important one for any brick-and-mortar business, not just a farm. When our friends at the Brooklyn butcher business The Meat Hook needed a commissary kitchen location for some of their more space-intensive work, they found one that fit the bill: it was near their butcher shop, and it was relatively turnkey. What it wasn't? Cheap. Fortunately, it happened to have a small street-facing storefront where they could run a business and create some revenue to help cover the cost. But instead of trying to put a full-service restaurant in the front of their commissary kitchen, for which the space was really too small, they created a sandwich shop. It fit nicely in the room, and helped offset the expense of the commissary operation, allowing them to be a bit more flexible in the projects they took on within the rest of the space. It was also reviewed by the *New York Times*, which meant a lot more business for both the sandwich shop and the butcher shop.

For a brick-and-mortar business, the space you choose and

its location are as important as the partners with whom you strike a deal, and flexibility of purpose is key to utilizing that space correctly. To that end, when striking a deal or expanding, it's important that your partners be flexible, too. We've been approached by landlords whose roofs are too small to farm commercially but are centrally located enough to attract a ton of visitors. If we were able to build a beer garden in the center of our farm, we could afford to operate in such a scaled-down location. But if the landlord is only interested in a farm and isn't flexible about what else that farm does to create revenue, he might not be the right partner for his own space. We keep an open mind and are willing to reshape our plans based on the opportunity that a particular space presents, but we're not going to try to fit a square peg into a round hole. We've learned to recognize a bad fit when we see one and to walk away.

We've seen a lot of our business-owner friends—especially those in the restaurant industry—waste a ton of time meeting with potential partners before realizing they're not a good fit. If the partner is across the country or halfway around the world, they've spent not just time but money, only to watch the deal collapse in the final stages. Not only do they wish they had that time and money back, but more than once we've heard our colleagues express regret at jumping the gun on announcing a partnership that later fell through. They say any press is good press, but it can be a blow to your brand to put out a release on an expansion deal, only to yank it down the road and hope nobody notices. We witnessed it happen to a fellow rooftop farm-ing business, and it taught us a lesson we won't soon forget.

This particular business launched in 2011 with a smart and innovative strategy, which they borrowed from the solar energy industry's PPA, or Power Purchase Agreement, model. Just as PPAs allow the owner of a solar array to maintain a system on a third party's property and then collect fees on the energy used by that property, the farm's CEO locked in contracts with supermarkets to purchase all of the greens grown in his urban hydroponic greenhouses ahead of time, before he'd even built out the farms. It's a rather ingenious move: the guaranteed rev-enue is an assurance to investors that they will see a return quickly, and it enabled the farm to raise more than $10 million over just a few years.

In the spring of 2012, they announced they would be install-ing a rooftop greenhouse atop a massive building in Brooklyn. We knew of the building but had heard from the broker re-presenting it that they wanted a crazy amount of rent, so we were impressed, if not surprised, when we heard the well-funded business had snagged the space. The media around the deal was dizzying: the ribbon-cutting ceremony alone was sig-nificant, complete with podium, microphone, and press pool, and attended by local politicians and celebrity chefs. The CEO announced that this was the first of many farms they expected to open in Brooklyn, and that they planned on moving quickly with their flagship build-out.

The greenhouse was not to be. We don't know for sure what happened with the deal, but we learned it wasn't happening when the broker called us a little over a year later and said the building's owners would be interested in speaking with us, in spite of the fact that we couldn't afford what our colleagues had been offering. Next we heard the business had installed a massive greenhouse in a rural area at ground level. The press release that had been so widely circulated about the Brooklyn rooftop project all but disappeared from the Internet. And though they now have a sizable growing operation and plans in the pipeline for another—what many would consider to be a huge success—their ground-level rural or peri-urban greenhouses will always be overshadowed for some by the rooftop urban operations they had promoted so heavily just a few years ago.

Before we announce a deal, we like to have a signed lease. Sometimes it's strategic to announce before signing because it can put pressure on both parties to execute. But the risk is big. Like name-yourself-for-Brooklyn-and-then-open-a-farm-in-Queens big. So if we were ever to announce a deal (again) before having a partner's signature, we would want to make sure that several important criteria were met.

First off, we always make sure we have the resources to deliver on a project before moving forward with it. If it would stretch us too thin financially, or if we would have to bloat our payroll in excess of the new revenue it would create to hire staff to manage it, we're not in a good place. When we signed the deal with the Brooklyn Navy Yard, it might have looked to an outsider like the wrong time: Gwen and I still hadn't started paying ourselves, and Ben was working way too much. But we had a solid roster of skilled folks who were chomping at the bit to work for us full-time, and we were confident we could create enough revenue with the increased growing space to hire a farm manager to help Ben and Gwen helm our respective locations, as well as put me on the payroll so I could quit my night job and generate increased income for us across the departments I managed.

The real key to the Navy Yard deal, however, was that it came with the lion's share of the funding we needed to cover the installation costs in the form of the DEP grant. While we knew we could create revenue to operate the project sustainably, it wouldn't have been a smart deal for us if we had to massively dilute our equity or raise an unhealthy amount of debt to get it off the ground. When Ben and Chase first met with the BNYDC, and they started listing the size of their available buildings, there was a moment of uncertainty: a lot of the sites, including the one on which we built, were huge, and we wondered how hard we should leverage our resources in order to expand. But with the support of the city—and our partners at the Navy Yard, who, if you'll recall from Chapter 3, contributed half the funds for those line items that weren't covered by the grant—we would have been fools *not* to move forward. Sure, we had to launch a second round of financing to raise our portion of the funds, but our investors were generally happier to see us expand than they were unhappy to own a slightly smaller share of our business.

Another aspect of the Navy Yard deal that attracted us to it was that our partners at the BNYDC shared our goals and visions for the project. They, too, were interested in seeing the farm built as an example of well-integrated green design and an opportunity to create green jobs. If they had only been interested in counting money with a shovel, we, with our modest margins and core tenets of social enterprise, would have been a disappointment, and if the deal had ever reached fruition, it would have resulted in an ugly butting of heads down the road.

It's also important that at least one person on the team be passionate about the project and excited to take the reins on getting it up and running. Of course, we operate as a team, and when we're launching a new enterprise, it's typically an all-hands-on-deck situation. But someone has to be prepared to really dive in. As Chase puts it, there should be an emotional stakeholder. Neither Gwen, Ben, nor myself were particularly excited about creating a commercial apiary at first. We didn't know how to keep bees, and although I've fallen in love with them since, I was downright terrified of them in those days. I couldn't even tend to the rows nearest the hives, which were left unplanted and became overrun with weeds (I guess I wasn't the only one). But Chase was determined to see the project come to life, and that determination carried him through the sweaty transport of hives up steep sets of stairs and the most painful stings.

Yet when we were in talks with the owner of a midtown building about building a farm on their roof—the one to which Ben showed up with the single boot, in fact—and we stopped hearing anything from them after a few months of trading proposals, we let it go. If one of us had been superexcited, we would have followed up until we received an answer. But we had a long list of reservations about whether we shared the same goals for the project as the developers, so when we realized it had been months since anyone had even asked Ben, who had been the main point of contact, what the status was, we knew: this wasn't the deal for us.

Far trickier is when one of us is enthusiastic about a project and the others feel it's not a good fit for the business. It's one thing if we're not unanimously motivated to work on it; one could argue it's actually better when a few members of the team aren't distracted by the new, shiny enterprise and can stay focused on current operations. But if there's a difference of opinion on whether the new project is good for the brand, that's another story entirely.

This has only come up once or twice. The Lower East Side

development was one such example of a project being potentially at odds with our brand. It was difficult for me, in particular, to swallow. As a native New Yorker, I'd grown up hanging
out in that neighborhood when it was a rich and vibrant community of mostly Hispanic families and artists, and I felt that
our attachment to the project—which some critics were por-
tending to be the nail in the coffin of any culture that remained
in the community—would generate negative feelings about our
business and paint us as gentrifying sellouts. Ultimately, I never
really had to state my case because the deal fell through. I was
patient, knowing that it might, and didn't waste my or our partners' time belaboring a point that ended up being a nonissue.
But it might have become a larger conversation if the deal had
progressed further.

There is a scenario we've had to hash out a few times that is
germane to this point: one of us is gung ho to buy a large tract of
rural farmland and expand our product offerings to include the
space-intensive crops that don't make sense to grow on a rooftop,
like corn and grain. We could use our existing office management and sales infrastructure, for the most part; we could employ a bunch more folks, and—though we haven't gone as far as
running the numbers—we could likely bring in a bit of revenue.
More than anything, though, it would be a strategic investment:
we'd hold on to the land and pay its property tax using the revenue we create until it appreciates. Land is never really a bad
deal. But given the fact that our brand is grounded firmly in the

land on which we plant—that is to say, *urban rooftop* land—it could dilute our brand to the degree that it undermines our core mission. If we were to buy rural ground-level land, it might be seen as a blow to what we've been arguing for so long: that it's possible to create a fiscally sustainable model for an urban agriculture business. So for the time being, we've decided, we need to keep working toward becoming synonymous with urban rooftop farming, and we still have to prove that the concept is viable. Buying rural land, while a smart investment, would make us less unique, and could hurt our argument in favor of investing in the creation of urban green space.

Reflecting on what we've learned in our mission to expand Brooklyn Grange, we realize that forging smart business partnerships is a lot like forging strong romantic relationships, and our advice to a budding entrepreneur might read like a love advice column. First off, know yourself. Figure out what's non-negotiable for you, and don't be afraid to communicate those points. Just like in a romantic relationship, you'll have to make compromises in order for any business partnership to work, but there are certain things that your business simply cannot live without. Figure out what those things are—no, really, make a list if you need to—and don't bend on them. We, for example, have walked away from otherwise perfect roofs because, while the owners are happy to have us up there farming, they refuse to let us host events or photo shoots. Those two revenue streams are just too important to our bottom line. If the roof were scaled up enough and the rent low enough, we might be able to make the model work on vegetable sales alone, but we've spent too much time and effort learning how to execute that angle of our business well—too many steps forward, as it were—to take a step backward and operate a small rooftop farm with vegetable sales as its only income.

Equally important to knowing your own priorities is understanding those of your potential new partner. If your expansion plans involve getting in bed with another entity, you'd better fully understand their motivation for wanting to work with you. If your motivation and their motivation are at odds with each other, you might still be able to strike a deal, but your partnership is not going to result in success. This might seem obvious, but when you're eager to get a deal done, mutuality can slip through the cracks easily. They want the deal, you might think, and we want the deal—so what could go wrong? But when we meet with a building owner who is really just looking for someone to maintain a beautiful green space on their roof so their tenants—sometimes thousands of people—have somewhere to go on their lunch break, we are wary. We have a business to run, and we can't do it if we're spending a chunk of time every afternoon answering people's questions about plants and cleaning up their sandwich wrappers. Instead, we might pitch

those building owners on a green roof installation and maintenance plan rather than a fully functional farm.

Of course, compromise is necessary. We've started including
in our proposals small gathering spaces for building tenants
to spend time because they are requested more and more often.
We don't want to lose out on a good deal because of some in-
tractable unwillingness to share the space. In fact, we love the
idea of our space being enjoyed by our neighbors, as long as
their presence doesn't come at the cost of our efficient operations. So we've figured out compromises wherein we can accommodate this increasingly frequent request without giving
away the farm, as it were.

That's where the similarities between romantic and business
partnerships end and the teeth come out. A bit of savvy is necessary in operating an organization, and if it doesn't come natu-
rally to you, don't worry too much: you'll find it emerges when
the business into which you've poured your blood, sweat, and
tears is on the line. You might think sharkiness is a product of
greed, but more often than not, the fiercest negotiators are simply the most protective of their company because they've worked
so hard to get where they are. You might have been sweet and
accommodating once, but the moment you witness manipula-
tive players trying to have their way with a venture that has
been a labor of love, you'll find your inner shark.

The first thing hard-nosed new you will learn to do is get

every pledge in writing. Potential partners will make you all sorts of promises: deliver on your end and we'll do this, that, and the other. Well, you won't have any leverage once you've delivered on your end, so make sure they've committed to their guarantees in a signed, sealed deal. There are certain things we won't discuss on the phone because we want it in an email, in writing.

All these lessons might be more pertinent to our company than, say, a tech start-up or a shoe store, but we've found while chatting with other small-business owners that there's more commonality than we expected. At the very least, there's one sentiment that seems fairly universal: starting a business can often feel like wandering blindly without a map. But as soon as you start generating income and cultural capital, roads will appear all around you. It's important for the operators of any venture to be thoughtful about which routes they choose to take, but even more important, never hesitate to turn around and double back if you don't like the direction you're headed. The more you know yourself, the more you understand your potential expansion partners, and the more you've thought through whether it's the right path for your company, the less likely you'll have to retrace your steps, which is never anybody's goal.

The Navy Yard deal was a well-lit and freshly paved street taking us in exactly the direction we wanted to go: the resources were in place, both financially and on the personnel front. Our partners shared our goals. Everyone on our team was excited about it. Just having access to the historic, and otherwise private, property was thrilling! And of course it was perfectly on brand: we could finally say that we had a farm in Brooklyn. It was a no-brainer. One of the only downsides is that it was such a good deal, it has made subsequent deals look paltry in comparison. The Navy Yard isn't perfect; the fact that the public cannot get past the gate without being registered as our guest, for example, means we can't have an open-house day for the community to enjoy the farm, like we do at our flagship rooftop. The bathrooms are a mess, and the hallways are lifeless and institutional. We often joke about the fact that, whereas we have to clean up after an event at the flagship farm, at the Navy Yard, we have to clean up beforehand. The freights are painfully slow, and there's always a queue of manufacturing tenants loading out huge shipments. But the deal was advantageous enough that we're a bit spoiled now.

A better way of putting it is that expanding to the Navy Yard opened our eyes to nonnegotiable needs we didn't previously know we had. (Hell, slow or not, we're thrilled to have direct freight access at the Navy Yard!) With those priorities now clearly articulated, it's become more difficult to convince ourselves that a less favorable deal is worthy of our investment. But while the Navy Yard may have slowed our roll on expanding to new locations, it didn't stop us from hitting our financial goals. We are generating more revenue on the two rooftops we cultivate today than we'd projected we would realize from seven such spaces. This is because the best deals we have made over the last five years have been with our staff, in whom we invest and who have invested themselves fully in our business.

Their passions and skills have allowed us to expand to new enterprises without having to expand our footprint. The diversity of our revenue streams is only made possible by the diversity of the folks who manage them. The People page of our Web site could go head to head with the rosters at some of the best consulting firms in New York, and our staff could out-charm a political candidate during election season. But as owners, we will take some credit: we've passed along the lessons we've learned in making deals to the team. Everyone who is responsible for making Brooklyn Grange thrive from season to season is strategic and savvy. That is how we've managed to grow one company on two rooftops into what are arguably three symbiotic businesses: a productive vegetable farm, a venue for private events and public programming, and a designer and builder of urban green spaces.

8

THE WEB WE WEAVE

Fifty Ways to Stay Afloat

Sometimes a word will gain traction in the collective lexicon—especially now, in the digital age—and seem perfectly apropos for a bit, before it's listicled and bait-clicked to death and loses all meaning. We've used a few such words over the years to describe the array of operations and revenue streams that collectively make up Brooklyn Grange. "Prismatic" was once a go-to, but now it elicits eye rolls from the peanut gallery at our team meetings. We used to say we "activated" our spaces in every conceivable way. Now there are scare quotes around the A Word, and the eye rolls are accompanied by snoring sounds. "Cephalopod-like" just makes us sound like a giant octopus, though it does aptly depict the various arms of our business. There's the classic "diversified revenue streams," but if we use that term, we might earn actual snores. "Three-ring circus" might be the most accurate description.

Unfortunately, the most overused of the lot is also the most appropriate to describe why we've chosen to branch out into seemingly disparate but inseparably linked divisions of our business, and that's "sustainability." It's a shame that the word has been sucked dry of meaning by brands making empty claims about their corporate responsibility, because when used correctly, it's an elegant principle and a difficult word to replace. And it has everything to do with how we've managed to succeed at a humble undertaking in the most expensive, competitive city in the world.

From the beginning, we understood we would need to derive income from sources other than produce sales. Remember, we had Ben's yield data from Eagle Street Rooftop Farm when we were planning ours, and we knew that, unless we wanted to sell our veggies for prices that would only be appropriate if they were dipped in gold, we wouldn't be able to afford the start-up costs, let alone the overhead, of farming on a roof in New York City without getting creative. We didn't anticipate, however, just what a huge and essential part of our business each of our various departments would become. None of our enterprises could exist without the others; each one has, at some point, supported another when it has faltered or needed a leg up to grow.

We might have realized this sooner if we hadn't been distracted by another oft-used term in that first year: "The Future."

When we first started telling people about our plans to build the world's largest rooftop farm, we were overwhelmed by media inquiries. It was a great problem to have, but it also put a lot of pressure on us to define ourselves when we were still young. So it's no surprise that the way we described our company's mission was influenced by the more powerful voices around us. When we heard from the umpteenth person that we were "the future of farming," that our rooftop farms would cover the "cities of the future," we started, in spite of ourselves, to believe it.

We've never worn rose-colored glasses regarding the capacity of rooftop farms to feed entire cities. Anyone who tells you that's a viable model is either blowing smoke or just hasn't thought it through. Urban land is so scarce and so valuable that, especially when it comes to space-intensive foods such as grains, legumes, dairy, and meat, there's no way we can be self-sufficient without razing cities as we know them and rebuilding them from scratch or completely restructuring the human diet. So we're a little ashamed to admit that, as well-meaning, hopeful people—from journalists writing newspaper articles to Kickstarter supporters, even our families and friends on social media—began touting us as "changing the way the world grows and eats food," we let the hype distract us. We believed that our concept was only successful if it was replicated rapidly and widely, which is what led us to project an expansion plan as aggressive as seven farms in five years. Our misguided mission to prove the believers right caused us to measure our success in unreasonable, global terms.

When we finally got our business up and running, we still found ourselves listening to how others defined our mission, but this time, we were listening to a different set of voices. Rather than the international community of the Web, chumming digital waters with provocative clickbait about massive change and futuristic urban overhaul, we started listening to our customers. After all, these were the folks buying our food and making it possible for us to continue growing it.

Our customers were the folks in our community, the people who shopped at our farm stand, and those who showed up to see if we needed a hand shoveling out rows. And what they wanted had nothing to do with cities halfway around the world. It had to do with them and the roof on which we stood. It had to do with *our* city, but more specifically, with our borough, with our neighborhood, with the block, with the building. It had to do with access and education. It had to do with increasing urban green space, yes, but not by putting commercial farms on every rooftop. These folks didn't care if we ended up franchising our name in a few years and using drones to drop supersacks of soil on every roof in town. They wanted to know how they could get their tomatoes to look as healthy as ours, or whether their daughter's second-grade class could come up for a visit. They wanted to know whether they could be a part of this neighborhood farm. If you build it, they will come, but if you don't have anything to share with them when they get there, forget building fifty, a hundred, a thousand more. Before we could focus on the future, we had to capitalize on the opportunities we had before us, and our customers were telling us quite clearly what those opportunities were—and what they weren't.

It was a combination of community-minded enterprise and straight-up necessity that brought us to where we are today, with distinct but interwoven divisions of our business. The community gives us clear direction about what they would like to see us doing, and by listening to them—by reading every email that comes in, by talking to our customers and the chefs to whom we sell—we understand the markets available to us. But we also have the security of leaning on one or two streams when a third falters. It means none of our revenue streams is exploited too heavily as a resource, which is how we keep our business sustainable—in every sense of the word.

As a small-business owner, you start with a well-thought-out plan, and you do the best you can to execute it. Often, you start simple: focusing your energies on one thing you do well. If you're smart, however, you realize that things change. A once-robust market might vanish, or some other setback might threaten your business. So instead of focusing on one thing as you expand, you foster the growth of a few. Sony, for instance, would have gone out of business long ago if it had only made Walkmans. But because it specializes in several different products and is constantly updating its technology to stay ahead of—or at least keep up with—the curve, it maintains a steady business. Farming is one of the most vulnerable businesses you can get into, and many farmers aren't as fortunate as we are to have as many secondary and tertiary opportunities to create revenue as we do, since they lack the dense, diverse customer base we enjoy. We're incredibly privileged in that regard: if a hurricane comes through and destroys our crops one season, we might have to significantly scale back our expenses, but we wouldn't go bankrupt.

We started as farmers, and that continues to be the backbone of what we do, but our additional revenue streams—primarily events and design and installation, but also speaking and talent engagements, third-party tours, commercial photo and film shoots—are vital to the health of our business. There's a common bit of business advice floating around urging businesses to "productize your services." It means to take a service that you offer on a custom by-request basis—say, consulting, or customer service—and create a product of it: package it up, bullet point what it includes, make it easily digestible, and slap a flat rate on it. Doing so allows you to save time communicating what you are able to offer to your customers, scale and streamline your services, and over time, really perfect that service as you perform it over and over again. We see the wisdom of this advice and have employed it with certain services, such as weddings, for example, for which we have a few different packages. But our overall strategy in launching our events and design and installation services was sort of the opposite of productize. Rather, we "servicized" our products.

We realized that people were drawn to what we were doing in a way that transcended our produce. Our customers' enthusiasm to support our business outpaced what we were selling, and people wanted to engage with us beyond buying a three-dollar bunch of kale. International visitors staying in hotel rooms without kitchens couldn't make use of our harvest but wanted to visit our farm just the same. We began to seek out creative ways to deliver our farm to more people, to harness our network's enthusiasm. People didn't just want to eat Brooklyn Grange vegetables, they wanted to *experience* Brooklyn Grange. So we invited them up and created experiences, or we brought the experience to them, recreated it on their own roof or backyard.

One of our first design and installation clients was a restaurant account in Manhattan. They weren't content to order produce from us: they wanted their customers to sit among the herbs and flowers with which their plates were garnished. They asked Gwen to come in and set them up with a backyard garden of their own. It was a successful project, though the small scale made for thin margins. But Gwen saw the potential and dove into the enterprise headfirst, adding a Design and Installation Services page to our Web site and prepping us with talking points to use in media interviews about our urban greenscaping offerings. Before we knew it, we were receiving calls to build everything from small planter gardens on terraces to shallow-soil sedum green roofs on private residences. From living walls growing herbs and vegetables on chain-link fences to dye plant gardens for the Fashion Institute of Technology, her projects really run the gamut.

Most calls come in because people see what we've built at the farm: they come for a tour, or pop by a farm stand, and see not only the physical space but the atmosphere, the culture we've created—and they want to recreate it for themselves. Perhaps they want a pastoral oasis to which they can retreat and feel far above the city. They want to be able to escape without traveling more than a few steps from their bedroom or desk. This was the case with the media group that hired us to put a garden atop their new headquarters in the spring of 2015. Perhaps it was the fun, vivid photos we were posting on our social media feed that enticed them to want their own photogenic vista for fashion shoots, or perhaps they attended a rooftop dinner and thought their office happy hours would rise to the next level if they took place in a sky-high sanctuary. Gwen obliged, outfitting them with a stunning green space, complete with a koi pond and a swing set.

On the other end of the spectrum, there are clients who see

how much food we are producing or the ecological benefits that our green roof offers to the building beneath us. One such organization was the developer of a low-income housing facility in the South Bronx. Faced with an influx of tenants in a relative food desert, they were eager to offer fresh food options to the families they would be housing. So they approached us, and Gwen wrote and won a DEP grant to build them a huge green roof, split between pollinator-friendly, low-maintenance sedum and grasses and nourishing vegetables. Residents who move in below will each have a plot of their own where they can grow edible crops to bring downstairs to their apartment kitchens for dinner.

Recently, she volunteered us to build a vegetable garden for the United Nations. We didn't make any money on that particular project, but we did it anyway because, thanks to Gwen's hard work in drumming up business and her careful attention to margins, her department's success has given us the latitude to take on a few break-even projects that we feel contribute to the greater good of our community. Now leaders from all over the world who visit the UN will see that urban agriculture is not only possible but actively flourishing!

You name it, we've built it. Gwen spends her days proving that it's possible to grow something anywhere you are and adding green space to our concrete maze. But she doesn't build alone. Perhaps what we like best about Gwen's determination to grow our design and installation services into a flourishing branch of our business is that she is able to create far more green jobs in doing so than we could on our two and a half acres. Job creation has always been a goal of ours, but there are only so many jobs that a farming business can bear. Until we scale up the farm, we can't really scale up the labor side of it. As Gwen scales up the green landscape of wider New York City, she also employs some amazing budding farmers who are then able to add green roof installation, or sub-irrigated planter construction, to the list of skills on their résumés.

The design and installation arm of our business wasn't the only one to get its start thanks to an inquiry from a restaurant account. A restaurateur helped us develop our events program as another source of revenue as well. It all started in our first season, when we were asked by our friends at bobo—the folks who hosted that early Manhattan fund-raiser—if we could return the favor and host a dinner of theirs. That first dinner was a blast, but we had zero infrastructure. Our table and chairs were a thrown-together mess of wooden boards and pallets, and we hadn't yet learned that candles in Mason jars, while a cute idea, are a joke when it comes to rooftop winds. We made a few hundred dollars for our troubles that night, which at the time was big money for us. But we also worked way too hard for it. We knew we could do better.

Like most of our ventures, we grew the program slowly,

reinvesting its profits in improvements to our space until we had something approximating a real venue. First, Ben and his friends designed a better table. Ben's carpenter buddy, Jake, got us a bunch of cedar, and the resulting table, built mostly by Ben, Gwen, and Gwen's husband, Christopher, is a thing of beauty: fifty feet long and six feet wide, it seats sixty-five people and is tucked among plants at the west end of the flagship farm. Next, I asked Gwen to design light posts from which we could hang string lights. She dumped some concrete in three-gallon buckets and sank poles in the middle, drilled a hole through the pole for hooks, and voilà! Light posts that wouldn't blow over!

There was still the sticky wicket of the ground around the table, which slopes downward. At first, we tried to solve the conundrum by building bench seating with longer back legs, but while the result was stable enough, sitting on the benches gave one the sense of being about to fall backward at any moment—especially after a few glasses of wine. So when we received a call from our friends who ran a recycled building materials depot telling us that the city was ripping up the Coney Island boardwalk and paving it over, we didn't miss a beat in agreeing to split with them a Dumpster of the Brazilian walnut. It wasn't cheap, but we now have a deck built from that wood around the perimeter of our table, and every time we walk the length of it to serve our guests, we get a bit of a thrill knowing that our footfalls are landing on a bit of New York City history.

Now that we had the infrastructure, we could ramp up our

events game. At first, we tapped our restaurant accounts to collaborate with us on dinners. This was the easiest way to keep our events legal; they could use their liquor license to apply for a temporary permit on our behalf. It was a lot of paperwork, but our restaurant partners were supportive, and we didn't have to worry that the New York State Liquor Authority was going to show up and shut us down.

Once we dialed in the liquor license protocol, we had to figure out the actual event part of it. My background is in hospitality, so I had a bit of a brazen attitude about the whole endeavor. At first, I worked on events pretty independently, though it was, like everything we did, a team effort, with Gwen helping out on the facilities side, and Ben often ferrying kegs around town and playing host while I ran about like a chicken with her head cut off. Sure, I had worked in hospitality, but no restaurant with a gas line and actual light fixtures and, oh, I don't know, four walls and a ceiling could ever have prepared me for producing events on a rooftop farm. Our very first private event, for the Prospect Park Conservancy, was a cocktail party for thirty-five people. They had a bare-bones budget, so we couldn't afford to bring in a catering partner. Instead, we served up food I'd made myself: a trio of crostini with farm veggies and local cheeses, beet borscht shooters, kale chips, baby carrots and radishes with salsa verde, and, for dessert, olive oil cake with Grange lavender cream. It was way too much for one person to take on, and I was kicking myself as I scrambled around prepping the food late into the night the day before the event. By the time the guests arrived, I had actually pulled it off and was feeling quite pleased.

And then, it got dark. I had, in fact, anticipated that the sun would set, and we'd strung lights on Gwen's handmade posts all around the table so our guests could mingle comfortably. But I'd completely failed to consider the plating station under the water tower. I had just finished plating the first of the three crostini when the curtain of darkness dropped, and hard. As I stood there having a full-blown meltdown, I heard a voice behind me.

"Hello, are you with the farm?"

I turned around to see a bearded man in his fifties, his long hair pulled back into a ponytail. He had knee pads strapped over his work pants and had brought his own garden spade, which was tucked into a tool belt around his waist.

"My name's John. I heard about what you guys were doing up here so I thought I'd stop by and see if you needed some help with anything."

Just as I thought my head would explode—who shows up at seven in the evening to farm?—I noticed it: around his graying hair an elastic band was fitted with exactly what I needed.

"Is that a headlamp?" I barked at him, lunging forward. He drew back and took it off reluctantly.

"Uh, yeah, it's—" Before he could finish his sentence, I was thanking him profusely and adjusting the strap to fit my skull.

We never did see Headlamp John again after that night. In my haste to get the food plated and served, I didn't have much time to chat, so we know nothing about him except that he saved me from total humiliation.

Not a month goes by without some near-disaster. Frankly, we probably wouldn't have an events program at this point if it weren't for Tiny Miracle, or as she is legally known, Michele. For the first two seasons that we hosted events, Team Tiny, as Michele and I began calling ourselves for our diminutive statures, produced more events and dodged more proverbial bullets than we can remember. There were windstorms, heat waves, cold snaps, unexpected showers, broken elevators, bee swarms, blown fuses, and guests who went to the wrong farm. But those memories pale in comparison to the sheer number of stunning sunsets, perfect breezes, wedding proposals, tear-jerking vows, impromptu dance parties, and mind-bendingly delicious dishes. By the end of 2013, we had a good handle on how to produce each type of event, from lunches and dinners to galas and weddings to concerts and film screenings. For the most part, though, we were still being reactive rather than proactive, booking events as people requested our space rather than executing our own ideas.

The problem with being reactive is that you're leaving money on the table. For every client who has the money to book out our entire space and hire a caterer to cook them and forty of their closest friends a birthday feast, there are countless folks who cannot afford to host a private event but would love to experience a meal on the farm. So we began producing our own events and selling tickets to them. They're still not cheap, but they're affordable to a greater cross section of the community, and we try to make sure we keep the cost as low as possible. Our favorite way to do so (and avoid the hassle of heavy load-ins and -outs in the process) is by nixing rented plates and silverware altogether. At our Butcher Paper Dinners, we line the table at the flagship farm with butcher paper, and then dump piles of food meant to be eaten by hand on top of it. We invite New York State brewers and vintners to pour their wine and beer and rope a DJ buddy into spinning some tunes. The result is one of the most fun ways you can spend an afternoon: a remarkably diverse mix of guests sits around passing one another crabs and crawfish, ribs and cornbread, or pieces of sandwiches that span the length of the table. It's a great event series because it gets people eating in a truly communal fashion, which in turn gets them chatting and breaking down social boundaries. What's more, there is zero waste: we simply roll up the butcher paper when everybody leaves and compost the entire mess.

When we signed the lease at the Navy Yard and found ourselves with a giant paved deck, we knew we were really in the swim. We had freight access, which makes loading rentals in and out a breeze. And this time, we left the space bare, so we could configure it any which way. That farm has become the bread and butter of our events program, and between the two roofs, we hosted 102 events in 2014 alone. The revenue is important, sure, but more than that we love them because they're a point of access for folks who might be more comfortable with cocktails and canapés than compost and carrot seeds. How else would Tyra Banks ever have visited (and tweeted that her tummy was "smizing")? It's a way of utilizing the farm to its fullest potential during as many hours of the day as possible. And although the events take a lot of hard work to produce, there is nothing like sitting atop a pile of rentals at the end of a long night, once all the stray glasses have been tracked down and the last caterer has loaded out, cracking a cold beer, and looking over the twinkling city skyline. In the silence of night, with grease-smeared legs swinging and the gentle breeze blowing in from the south, those are the moments we cherish. After opening up our home to a hundred new friends and experiencing the joy they take in discovering this place, it is all the more special to us. It is our farm, and we are proud to share it with the community.

Our workshops and ticketed dinners aren't as profitable as weddings and private events, but we continue to do them because they're fun and folks love them. Spending that much time on a labor of love, though, is a dangerous game. Yet if all Michele and Robyn did was book and execute corporate product launches, they wouldn't be willing to spend their summer weekends at work. The trick to your business having a healthy balance of passion projects and profit drivers is to make sure there are no loss leaders: everything you do must at least break even, and if it's not turning a profit, it has to contribute to the growth of something that is. When we lead a great compost workshop for $30 a ticket, and everyone leaves feeling really happy, there's a good chance one of those attendees will come to another event or send friends our way. Maybe they'll book an office retreat; maybe they're getting married in the spring and looking for a venue. Maybe their co-op is planning to install a rooftop farm of its own, and now we're getting hired for the job.

Everything we do works with everything else we do to make the other components work even better and more effectively. Beyond just contributing revenue, the events create ways for visitors to engage with the farm so the farmers aren't being interrupted by visitors popping up willy-nilly, which they used to do before we offered tours and events. The events staff helps to keep the farm looking tidy and beautiful for our guests, which in turn makes it a more pleasant place to work. And it's not just events: When Chase books our space for a shoot with a work boot company, he gets us all free gear. When Gwen builds a farm for a third-party client, she is able to try out the newest materials and methods, which in turn helps us become smarter, more efficient operators.

It can be tough, at times, to stay focused with the number of different directions in which we're pulled. And sometimes, we are literally pulled in different directions. It's not unusual for us to travel for a conference or speaking engagement. Those trips are an important way for us to establish ourselves as experts in our field, and help get the word out about what we're doing, but it can be exhausting and distracting to keep up with our workload while flying or driving across the country. So we value our time highly and charge for our presence and intellectual property. We are told at least twice a week that we should appear somewhere and share our insight for free because "it'll be great publicity." But the truth is, especially with the democratizing effect of digital media, we don't need to be somewhere in person to get the word out on what we do, and while it can be fun and exhilarating to see a new corner of the world and meet the farmers who feed it, it's taxing. To that end, we do charge for those engagements, and have created a small but steady revenue stream marketing ourselves as experts.

Even stranger, especially for camera-shy Ben, is when we find ourselves being asked to appear as "talent." Sometimes a brand will be putting together a spread on a new clothing line of durable outerwear and thinks we would make the perfect poster children for its wares. Sometimes a company planning a product launch or media event wants the Brooklyn Grange brand—and one of the faces behind it—to lend our cultural capital to its experience. We have to be careful about these opportunities, as we've been well into negotiations with small "sustainable" companies in the past, only to realize they were quietly bought by a huge corporate giant with despicable business practices half a decade before. We would never want to cheapen our own brand or behave hypocritically in order to score a deal, so we always do our due diligence.

Even as we've expanded the events and installation arms of our business, or find ourselves getting used to having our noses powdered and stray hairs smoothed for the cameras, we never lose sight of our foundation as a farm. After all, our business wouldn't exist without its agricultural core. Nobody would attend events on our roofs if there were no farms there; that's what makes the spaces unique—not to mention a beautiful backdrop for a wedding. Far fewer people would ask us to design their growing spaces if we didn't have two of the largest and most verdant such spaces in the city. So alternative revenue streams aside, we need to constantly optimize the farming operations.

Everyone, whether they've farmed a day in their life or not, understands that a farmer mitigates her risk by growing more than one crop. But simply growing a bunch of crops isn't strategic, either. We talked in Chapter 5 about the importance of collecting and analyzing data in order to be as efficient as possible, and this is how we ensure we're only growing produce that will actually make us money. Ben has spent a significant amount of time creating systems for recording planting and harvest data, and calculating yields of each variety that we grow and the resulting value per square foot of each crop. While we don't factor in every single cost to get an exact net value—for example, we don't go as far as to take into account the time it takes to bunch radishes or the cost of the rubber bands that we use to do so—we can get a pretty good idea of what each crop is worth to us by looking at our total sales for that crop—wholesale, retail, and CSA combined—and tracking how many square feet of it we planted over the course of the season, then dividing the sales by the planted area. We know, for example, that red tomatoes, which are sold for a few dollars less per pound than the funky-looking and popular heirlooms, still gross us more per square foot than their higher-value cousins because they yield more than twice as much fruit. We know that mixed greens and arugula beat out any other crop's value by almost 150 percent. We know that peppers are profitable, but that we can eke out an extra 250 percent on them by buzzing them into hot sauce. In so doing, we've also removed the urgency to sell the peppers promptly, because unlike fresh peppers, hot sauce is shelf stable. Plus, we get a bit of marketing help when stores put that Brooklyn Grange–branded bottle on their shelves.

Profitability isn't the only metric we use to gauge what crops stay in rotation. It's necessary to keep some lower-value items in the mix so we have a nice variety and so we don't get bored. Nobody wants to grow only four or five things or eat the same veggies day in and day out. Sure, the ruby red beefsteaks are higher yield than the heirloom Green Zebras, which are always the first to succumb to blight. But cutting into a Zebra, or a Cherokee purple, or a Pineapple bicolor, the juices sluicing from the vividly colored flesh, is a thrill that we won't deny ourselves or the people we feed. Beans take forever to pick and sell for a song, but when the weather hits just right and you pop one in your mouth straight off the vine, it's sweet as a breath of fresh clover. We're pragmatic businesspeople, but we're also hungry farmers, and our appetites govern at least some of our decisions; if they didn't, we wouldn't think about our crops as food so much as inventory.

With all that in mind, we devise our plantings for each upcoming season. As demand for a given item increases, we might increase the square footage we allocate to it. If an item falls out of favor or if another farmer is selling it at a price way lower than we could afford to, we'll strike it from the mix. Still other crops just don't perform well in our conditions, and if a product's quality doesn't reflect the standards we've set for the farm, it, too, will be nixed. The result is a seasonal rotation of about three dozen types of produce, a half dozen of which compose about two-thirds of our square footage and the other thirty crops forming a very long tail.

There's more to smart farming than simply ordering the right kinds of seeds. It's not just about what you grow, but about how you sell it—and that's true of almost any business that markets a product. We sell produce through three channels:

wholesale, retail, and CSA. Diversifying these channels allows us to protect ourselves from vulnerabilities. If flea beetles descend on our greens beds one season and munch so many holes in our arugula that it looks like a target practice sheet after a cadet's first day in training, we can't very well sell it to chefs who charge $12 a plate for a salad. Similarly, the mom-and-pop grocers who support us won't move a single Swiss-cheesy leaf if there's a box of beautiful, unmolested arugula on the refrigerator shelf right next to ours, which there usually is. Our CSA members, on the other hand, to whom I write weekly emails detailing the growing and harvest conditions as well as flavor properties, storage, and cooking tips, will happily buzz the perfectly tasty greens into a pesto and freeze them in individually portioned ice cube trays so they can enjoy their fresh flavor in winter. They might even serve the fresh greens as a salad at a dinner party, and regale their guests with tales of how their farmers struggled this season because they uncompromisingly refused to use chemical pesticides. That narrative might, for some, create a connection to the food that makes it even more delicious.

Having a diverse range of sales channels is a smart practice, but a business's sales strategy shouldn't be all defense. Beyond growing an optimized selection, driving sales through the correct channels is essential to realizing the full value of our products. Take our basils, for example. We grow several different types, and none would be worth the water we use to irrigate them if we weren't selling them to the right customer. First, we've got Genovese basil. This is the sweet Italian basil that you see at every Stop & Shop and Piggly Wiggly across America. Home cooks know it and they love it. Chefs can get it from huge ground-level rural farms for about $5 per pound. If we were to sell sweet basil for that price, we wouldn't be able to afford to grow it, so we wholesale ours for $9 per pound, and chefs and grocers don't usually bite at that price. But the standard retail pricing for sweet basil is around $2 or $3 for a bunch that weighs around one-tenth of a pound. That adds up to a lot more per pound than we would ever be able to get for it at wholesale, plus it flies from our market table, and our CSA members love to receive a bunch of it to garnish their caprese salads come tomato season.

Speaking of CSA members, our favorite basil to stock in their shares is opal basil, the dark purple variety that tastes similar to sweet basil but has a bit of a heartier leaf. It doesn't wilt and rot as quickly as its green counterpart, making it a perfect choice for folks who don't want to have to supplement their share with store-bought basil after a few days. You can also substitute it in recipes for sweet basil, making it easy for our CSA members to adopt it into their cooking routines.

Then there's the lime basil. Lime basil is a small-leafed, tropical-scented herb. We've heard its aroma compared to that of green apple Jolly Ranchers, Fruity Pebbles, and lychee nuts. Its flavor profile shares almost nothing in common with sweet

basil, and it would be downright weird to top spaghetti al po-
modoro with its floral, exotic-tasting leaves. When we bring it
to market, we muddle a few leaves to draw people to our stand,
its aroma like a siren song. People smell it and stop dead in their
tracks: "What is that smell?" they ask us. We hand them a sprig,
tell them a bit about it, suggest they use it on a melon salad or
in a Thai lettuce wrap, and they nod enthusiastically. Then
they buy the sweet basil every single time.

People want things they know how to use. Even our CSA
members don't want lime basil more than once, maybe twice a
season. If we bring just six bunches with us to market, we'll
bring home at least four, and we'll end up making less on
our lime basil than we would wholesaling sweet basil. But you
know who knows how to use lime basil? Pastry chefs and bartenders. And they can't get it easily—or at least not with the
freshness of ours. So we can wholesale our lime basil for a higher
price than we can get for it at retail, and we'd be fools not to.

In addition to being selective about where we sell which
crops, we also eke out greater return by planting crops that have
multiple marketable parts and stages. Squash blossoms are a
great example. Zucchini itself is a relatively low-value, high-
maintenance vegetable, susceptible to all sorts of pests and diseases. Still, we find that it's worth growing, in small amounts,
because we get a secondary sale on squash blossoms, which
wholesale for as much as a quarter a piece and retail for even
more.

An even better example of a double-revenue crop was the result of a happy accident. Back in 2012, Ben, Gwen, and I were doing a farm walk, and I was trailing behind a bit, mostly listening. I'd just quit my bartending job to focus full-time on the farm and had taken over our sales program; Gwen had left Roberta's to manage the flagship farm so Ben could give all his attention to the Navy Yard. I knew if I didn't significantly increase revenues, Gwen and I wouldn't be able to draw a salary, so the wheels were whirring away in my head as we strode down row after row debating whether to yank the low-yielding pest-magnet strawberries altogether to make room for something more profitable.

When we got to the cilantro, Ben and Gwen both shook their heads at the spindly plants, which had bolted in the heat and gone to seed. As they were chastising themselves for being so behind that they hadn't yet pulled and reseeded that row, I narrowed my eyes and cocked my head. "Guys," I said, "I think I have an idea." Walking over to the row, I plucked one of the tiny, shiny, avocado-green orbs from the clusters that sprang from each branch and popped it in my mouth. The taste was at once familiar, and yet unlike anything I've ever encountered: fruitier and more floral than dried coriander but with all the herbal complexity, that same slight bitter note on midpalate, and a surprising citrusy finish. "Holy shit!" I exclaimed. "Yeah, I definitely have an idea."

We sold $200 worth of fresh, green coriander seeds in 2012,

and that was when we were still dumb enough to charge like drug dealers by the ounce and pick each individual berry off the stem. Midway through the following season we started charging by the stem and just cutting lower on the branch, which saved us a ton of time and meant the chefs got some flowers, too—and chefs love flowers. Chefs also talk to one another, and word had gotten around. We sold $1,250 worth of coriander berries in 2013. Restaurants were begging us for it because they couldn't get it anywhere else. By late 2013, one of the chefs we worked with mentioned that Lancaster, the cooperative of Amish farmers in Pennsylvania, had added it to their own price list at the same rate we were charging. Normally, when we didn't know what to charge, we checked Lancaster and some of the other area farms. It was one of our proudest moments when we realized that they were doing the same thing with our price list.

And with good reason: we're exceptionally adept at selling to chefs. After the coriander discovery, we started paying attention to the other "tweezer food"—what we call any garnishes that chefs apply to a dish with a pair of tweezers—that was growing on the farm. Wood sorrel, for example, is a weed that pops up in damp areas. It also happens to be a favorite garnish among chefs who plate prettily, and they were eager to add a small bag of it to their order. That small bag can increase a sale by 10 to 12 percent.

Our close relationships with—and physical proximity to—

the chefs with whom we work have given us useful insight into their needs, which helps us direct our own operations toward profitability. Realizing that most chefs were having microgreens—the small shoots of plants grown very densely in trays and used as a garnish—shipped from a farm in Chicago, we began growing them in our greenhouse in the off season. Over time, and with no small amount of research and trial and error, our farm manager, Matt Jefferson, has become a skilled and knowledgeable microgreens grower, and has created a profitable enterprise that brings in revenue all year long—something we hadn't previously enjoyed.

It can be dizzying keeping track of the complexities of a farming business, let alone the countless other revenue streams we've developed. The trick to managing the many divisions of our business is that we have a core. All three departments use a centralized communications, accounting, and office management team, which is efficient, because in a business as small as ours, none of them could afford me independently to do their PR, or Melissa, our CFO, to keep their books and order them office supplies. Hell, they could barely afford their own office space in this town, let alone their own office manager!

Melissa is truly amazing at keeping everything orderly. She's a miracle worker, because the complexity and nuance of Gwen's job expenses, the events expenses and commissions, the shared expenses across the company, and the sheer volume of produce, tours, and other invoices that we generate are mind-boggling. Though Melissa doesn't directly generate revenue, if it weren't for her, we'd all be less productive because we'd have to do that work on our own. More pertinent, we'd have no idea which areas of our business were the most profitable and which were loss leaders. Ben used to spend as much time as he could eke out on those calculations, but often by the time he got a chance to analyze the financial data of our business, the bleeds had already cost us. It's impossible to quantify how Melissa has improved our profitability, and we try never to take her hard work for granted.

Another difficult contribution to quantify is the work that Chase and I do on communications and external affairs. I love writing, so penning a blog post—or a book—can seem like more fun than work. Chase spends a good chunk of time on social media, and lord knows what folks must think when they see him hanging around with his feet up, snapping photos and brainstorming hashtags. But when we started asking the question "How did you hear about us?" on our events request form, it became clear just how important that work is. All revenue streams benefit from a coherent and visible brand. When we post a beautiful picture of a previous natural dye workshop on Instagram to advertise a future date, we sell out the class. When we do international media for a European audience, we are invited to speak at international conferences and are often offered a speaking fee, which we gladly take in the lean winter months. When we participate in an article on how to build a home garden and point out that we offer design build services, guess what happens?

Sometimes it all seems incredibly complicated. There are days when we envy our colleagues at Gotham Greens, the hydroponic rooftop farming business that only grows, packages, and sells lettuce, basil, and, as of recently, tomatoes. They have no weddings to set up for, no rental companies wheeling dollies through their grow labs. They don't have prospective clients taking photos of them as they harvest. We didn't choose that route because our business, unlike theirs, is seasonal, and we'd be broke if we had. But we'd also be downright bored. We have no doubt that the innovative minds behind Gotham Greens keep themselves plenty busy with the complexities of their own operation and their developing industry. But that's not what makes us tick.

Because among the other things the branches of our business afford us is the almost constant interaction with our community. At the end of the day, it is the time we spend with the people on the farm that we love the most. Money is not the only metric by which we measure our success. We've dedicated a lot more words in this book to discussions of striking deals and raising revenue than anything else for the simple fact that, without fiscal stability, our business—and any small, ambitious venture—would crumble. But though we weigh all our company's priorities against their capacity to earn income, we do make the calculation. And as a triple-bottom-line business, money doesn't always come out on top.

Our cultural capital is of greater value to us than our bank balance. The relationships forged on our rooftops, the lessons learned, the hope regained, the vows made . . . these are the things we feel most deeply and profoundly. So while, thus far, we've largely focused on running a profitable business, that's only because we've had to illustrate the difficulty of being shrewd when you're chasing a dream. But we wouldn't give one red cent about any of it if it weren't for the connectivity that the farm affords with the community around us.

9

IT TAKES A VILLAGE

The Partnerships
That Make Us Whole

Ask any of our staff what their favorite thing about Brooklyn Grange is, and chances are, they'll tell you it's the people. They're not just referring to their coworkers, though. Brooklyn Grange hosts not only our own team but several other organizations who call our roofs home, and each of them brings something incredible to the farm.

There's City Growers, the educational nonprofit, which was founded in 2011 and has since brought more than fourteen thousand New York City youths to our roofs to learn about food and farming. There's the Refugee and Immigrant Fund, which provides asylum seekers, refugees, and immigrants with job-readiness skills and English-language immersion through on-farm training. There's Brooklyn Mompost, the business of local mother, nutritionist, and master composter Dr. Annie Hauck-Lawson, who maintains a compost operation on the corner of the farm that she sublets from us. Professor Mark Hellerman might pop up with the City Tech student garden club to tend to their beds at any moment, and Yoshi is always running around tinkering with his sensors, a blur of black clothing in the blazing sun. Just when you think the clown car couldn't get any more crowded, here comes Get Up and Ride bike tours, with twelve headset-clad Dutch tourists in tow. It's a circus, to be sure, and we wouldn't have it any other way.

In the past few years, companies have started referring to their followers on social media as their "community." But to us, community means something else. Media saturates our everyday lives, especially in cities. Even when we are in close quarters on crowded streets and subways and in packed cafés, we're on our phones, we're listening to music, we're swiping left and right in the hope of meeting someone instead of looking up and around at the very people with whom we are sharing space. Less and less often are we confronted with the physicality of our fellow humans.

At Brooklyn Grange, everyone gets introduced in real time, and fast. The farm makes you acutely aware of the bodily presence of others: their feet navigating around yours on the narrow path between beds, the flex of their forearm muscle as they hand you a case of zucchini, the smell of their sweat and sunscreen, and the tomato tar blackening their fingers. In a sense, the roofs we cultivate provide a kind of refuge from the alienation of city life in the digital age. Brooklyn Grange is a space for face-to-face conversation: even the shyest farmers have to ask questions when they're new and still learning, and one simple query on a farm can come with a lengthy explanation. And when you spend forty-five minutes picking foul-smelling squash beetles off vines across from a relative stranger, you'll chat about almost anything to distract your brain from the task at hand.

Beyond connecting those who are cultivating the roofs, the farm gets others talking, too: when we step into the elevator, our neighbors often chat us up about what's growing during the long ride to the top floor. The guests at our Butcher Paper Dinners are forced to acknowledge the folks sitting across from them when they can't reach that ear of corn or that bottle of Grange hot sauce. We've seen the simple act of one stranger passing a crab to another, holding its leg with bare Old Bay–smeared hands, turn into an exchange of contact info and a promise to keep in touch.

The farm is all about interaction and fostering community. It is, we all realize, the most special thing about it, and gives us our greatest chance to make a socially significant impact. We understand how important this opportunity for physical gathering is; we don't want our children growing up unable to read facial cues because their social interactions are limited to clicking through frozen Facebook smiles. So we relish our role as a gathering place for those in our network.

At the same time, we have a business to run, so while we want to make sure we're not squandering the chance to foster meaningful connections in our space, we also don't want our operations to devolve into a big party. We've got work to do! If we wanted to party all day, we would've just opened a bar! Rather, we want to create a social dimension of productivity and innovation; we want to engage in the kind of problem solving that's best done with more than one head put together. To that end, we're strategic about the partnerships we establish. We seek out—and are often sought out by—like-minded organizations that foster positive communities of their own, and we welcome them to join our circus.

Consequently, the network of organizations that call our rooftops their home base is as diverse as our revenue streams, though revenue doesn't always factor into our motivation behind forming relationships with our partner organizations. We have figured out how to create revenue on the farm; as entrepreneurial operators, that's something we're good at. So while everyone who uses the farm as a place of business has to help keep the lights on, so to speak, by covering the value of the space or time they take up, the strategy behind the partnerships to which I'm referring has nothing to do with money and everything to do with community.

Forging strategic partnerships is an essential way for any business to accomplish more than they would be able to if they were acting alone. Look at the rising popularity of coworking spaces, wherein independent contractors and the self-employed share communal office space. Sure, a big part of the traction that concept has gained comes from bloated rents and increasing overhead costs of doing business. But most of its proponents will tell you their favorite element of joining the community of a coworking space is just that—the community! These coworkers are not employed by the same people and often work in wildly different fields, yet they share values, and that is the only bond they need to coexist successfully and productively. They might recommend one another for jobs, or lend an objective set of eyes to a project in process. Perhaps the graphic designer sitting at the next desk ends up illustrating the writer's next book, and the event producer plans the launch party!

Similarly, the physical locality of our business, its function as a venue for people to interact in real life, is what draws our particular community in, but it's our shared values that keep us working together. While it'd be nice to believe that everything we do is perfect, we are well aware that we have areas at which we do not excel. By creating bonds with like-minded organizations who specialize in our weaker areas, we are able to serve a greater number of people. Case in point: Back in 2010, when we started receiving our first requests for tours, we were thrilled that a few schools expressed interest in bringing students to the farm. At first, it was mostly the private school teachers who had the time and luxury of researching field-trip options, and they all offered compensation, assuring us they had a budget for these things. Great, we thought, another revenue stream! And so I started touring kids around the farm, developing games and lessons using the roof as a learning laboratory.

Then we received our first request from a Title 1 school, which is the Department of Education's designation for elementary and secondary schools that are improving the academic achievement of the disadvantaged. These schools are mostly broke public schools that sometimes don't even have the budget for books, and the families of the students that go there often can't afford even a modest field-trip fee. So we made an exception and offered the school a pro bono visit.

It was during this visit that we received an early lesson in just how crucial environmental education is in urban areas—and we got a great story to boot. The kids in this group were around ten or eleven years old, from a public school in the Bedford-Stuyvesant section of Brooklyn—a working-class neighborhood best known for its slogan "Do or Die Bed-Stuy." They were, for the most part, wide-eyed with wonder at this acre of farmland on top of a building they'd most likely pass off on first sight as a boring old place for grown-ups to go to work. When I asked them if they were learning about food and farming in their classrooms, they all shook their heads.

"But I bet you're learning about the environment, right?" I asked, ready to hammer home the connection.

"Yeah, but the environment has nothing to do with us," offered a boy near the back of the group.

"What do you mean?" I asked.

"That's out there," he replied, gesturing off the roof somewhere toward the horizon.

"Out where?" I countered, genuinely confused as to where he was referring. All I could see was the rail yard full of trains awaiting repair.

"Out there!" he exclaimed, eyes rolling at my thickheadedness. "In the country! Where there's trees and stuff!"

I laughed—how could you resist? It was an adorable moment, getting that child's view of the world. We forget as we get older that the planet seems tiny to a child, or at least it does to a little New Yorker. After all, at what point in his average day is he confronted with the world outside his vast metropolis? What reminder does he have of the fact that these products and goods, so readily available to him, come from somewhere other than the corner bodega? What about his life suggests to him that his behavior has anything to do with "the environment"? With more than half the world's population now living in urban centers, this is the reality faced by the majority of children growing up today. Many of these kids will spend their formative years waking up in the morning, descending from their apartment building down into the subway, which they'll take to their concrete-block schools, where they'll spend their days looking out a window at a whole mini-universe of other concrete blocks.

How can we expect the next generation of urban dwellers to understand that their choices—the way they consume resources and products and dispose of waste—have any impact whatsoever on the larger global ecosystem?

We loved the idea that we could radically alter these kids' perceptions of the world around them and their relationship to food, so we made another exception for another Title 1 school that wanted to come to our roof but couldn't afford the fee. After making ten more exceptions, we realized it was going to take us more time than we had to serve the youth who needed our farm the most.

But we don't let a challenge intimidate us, so we scheduled a meeting to discuss the future of our education program. It was early spring 2011, shortly after Gwen had given birth to her eldest son, Otto, and it was the first time any of us had met him. Perhaps we all felt a bit parental that day, faced with this sweet little babe. But when Gwen suggested that we forego the income from our youth visits in favor of creating a real program that had the capacity to reach the kids most in need, we rallied behind her. It didn't make sense to treat youth education as a revenue stream, the way we did with, say, vegetables. Vegetables are a *product* for which there is a market; educating children is a *service* of which the community deserves to be able to avail itself.

Also, the truth is, I had zero background as an educator, and I was totally making it up as I went along. Some days, my attempts at being an educator were more successful than others, such as my lesson on chicken anatomy, in which I used a mortar and pestle and a bowl full of lemon juice to replicate a chicken's digestive system. Other days, I was asked questions like "But how do the chickens lay eggs without a rooster?" and was doubly flummoxed when, looking up at the teacher for help, I was met by a quizzical expression (one teacher actually seconded the query: "Yeah, how *do* they lay the eggs without a rooster?"). But while we easily could have hired some AmeriCorps graduate to helm our educational division and continued to collect the service fees from the schools that could afford to pay them, we believed that would be doing a disservice to our community. So Gwen initiated the long and arduous process of applying for a 501(c)(3) designation, the IRS's classification for tax-exempt nonprofits, to form a distinct organization: the educational nonprofit, which we called City Growers.

City Growers was fortunate to find early support from a woman named Ellice Lee, whom Ben had met while volunteering for a mentoring program. Gwen, Ellice, and I worked hard to establish by-laws for City Growers. It's a lot of legwork creating an organization, even one—perhaps *especially* one—that doesn't pay taxes, because the government insists on a whole lot of documentation that the work being done is worthy of tax exemption. For example, the first application Gwen put together for the IRS made it through months of the initial review process before it was rejected because it was missing a clause stating that, in the event of dissolution, we would return all assets to the community. We were forced to start from scratch. To make matters more complicated, the IRS pays special attention to nonprofit organizations that have very close ties to for-profit businesses, like we did with City Growers. They want to make sure we're not forming charitable arms, taking donations on which we don't have to pay taxes, and using that money to pay employees who are actually working for the commercial arm.

It took about a year, but eventually the organization was formed and incorporated with the government. In the meantime, I'd raised some money through fund-raising events, and we partnered with an existing nonprofit organization to act as a "fiscal conduit"—an intermediary through which we were allowed to take donations while our legal status was still pending. By the time City Growers was officially a registered 501(c)(3) entity, Ellice had recruited a healthy board, Gwen had written a successful grant proposal, and we were ready to hire someone to take over our nascent organization.

That person was the very capable Cara Chard. A former New York City public school teacher, Cara had a great handle on the mind-sets of the kids coming up to the farm. As a relatively new beekeeper, she was herself experiencing the wonder of someone being exposed to an aspect of the natural world for the first time. As executive director of City Growers, Cara has, like us cofounders of Brooklyn Grange, spent time filling every role in the organization, from educator on up. But perhaps what qualified her best was the fact that Cara was mother to her own little city grower, Zadie Faye.

When Cara was hired to run City Growers in early 2012, Zadie was two. Since then, she's been up to the farm almost weekly, and has become as comfortable on our rooftops as any of us cofounders. When Cara brings her along to a farm function, Zadie barely misses a beat before tugging on her mother's sleeve to announce, "Mama, I'm just gonna go say hi to the worms." Often, she'll then turn to whoever is standing nearest and, much to their surprise, offer to introduce them to the red wrigglers writhing around in the compost. Then, with the confidence of a farm manager, she'll walk the rows and check on all the crops, declaring the name of each one proudly and making comments aloud about their progress: "That's nice Swiss chard!" and "Those are the peppers. Some are hot!" But perhaps more than the worms, or the bees, or even the chickens, Zadie loves greens of all flavors, and before departing will usually head to the educational bed that City Growers rents from Brooklyn Grange to collect "some leaves for the road."

Perhaps what is particularly inspiring about Zadie's attitude toward the farm is how completely nonchalant she is. It's even more inspiring when contrasted with the alienation expressed by Trees and Stuff. Zadie is an anomaly, but she doesn't have to be.

When city kids come to the farm, they unlearn more than they learn. A farm field trip is a process—as Cara always says—of debunking myths: the myth that soil is dirty and needs to be cleaned, that vegetables are gross, worms are icky, bees are terrifying, and all insects are grounds for calling the exterminator. Most of these kids have only ever encountered bed bugs, fleas, lice, and cockroaches, or maybe an errant ant problem. So to impress upon them that worms, bees, ladybugs, and praying mantes are friends of the farmer and should be welcomed with open arms, not swatting hands, is never an easy lesson. But almost every group that has come to the farm has left convinced that worms are essential to building healthy soil and bees are critical to producing healthy food. Of course, it doesn't help when, immediately after the kids are done digging through the worm bin for red wrigglers, squealing with glee as they pass the squirming night crawlers from student to student, their well-meaning teacher calls them over to line up and disinfect their digits with a squirt of antibacterial solvent.

Yet not even the most germophobic teacher can tame the sheer hysteria of a group of children pulling a carrot from the ground for the first time. Their excitement can be heard from across the farm, and often emerges in the form of screams so bloodcurdling, one would think they'd been thrown over the parapet wall. But no, all it takes is an eight-inch tuber plucked from the bed and dangled before them and kids are beside themselves with a thrill usually reserved for celebrities or the release of the newest video game. Another classic is a student's first taste of lemon sorrel. Often referred to in thank-you notes as "lemon swirl," and even "squirrel," this tart green leaf is a real black horse. Who would have thought that young palates would be so enamored of a crop that most adults find mouth-puckeringly sour? Yet it is hands down the favorite crop of every child who visits Brooklyn Grange.

Helping these kids discover an enthusiasm for vegetables might just seem like we're doing a solid for the parents of picky eaters, but it's so much more than that. A lot of the kids who visit the farm come from single-parent homes, homes where both parents work—sometimes multiple jobs—or, worst of all, homes where their parents cannot find work. These families are struggling, and when they go food shopping on a budget so small they're worried it won't cover a full week of meals, you can bet they're not going to buy a salad for their kids. They're focused on making sure their children get enough calories so they don't go hungry, and nine times out of ten, they're going to get a package of preformed burger patties and a bag of buns. And we've seen the results of what happens when kids lack proper nutrition; it's not unusual to see one kid in a group visiting from a particularly rough public housing project who's a few inches shorter than his classmates; sometimes he'll have a cast on his arm or leg, where a bone deprived of calcium has become too fragile and fractured. More often than not, he's stuffing his pockets with cherry tomatoes and cucumbers when nobody is looking.

Seeing kids suffering from hunger is heartbreaking, and as business owners, Ben, Gwen, Chase, and I often have conversations asking ourselves if we can be doing more to help combat this problem. But at the end of the day, we have rent to pay, and while we'll turn a blind eye to a hungry kid sneaking snacks when he thinks no one is looking, we can't do something truly impactful, like donate our harvest to a food bank, or we'd never be able to pay our employees, our rent, and our insurance, which makes the education work we do possible. We can't solve every problem plaguing this city, so we focus on what we know we can do well: improving the environment and increasing public awareness of food and farming issues through education and advocacy work. That's why we try to identify and forge strategic partnerships wherever we can to assist the organizations that are making strides in those areas in which we fall short. That's the beauty of our relationship with City Growers: they don't have to worry about engaging structural engineers, building greenhouses, or maintaining landlord relationships; that's what we do. And in turn, we leave to them the incredibly valuable and crucial job of educating tomorrow's eaters.

———

For the participants of another organization that calls Brooklyn Grange its home, the fact that there is a farm on the roof of a building is just one uncanny aspect in a life full of strangeness. The refugees, asylum seekers, and immigrants who are part of the Urban Farm Recovery Project led by the Refugee and Immigrant Fund (or RIF, for short) often arrive in America alone, having fled their native countries and lost their families in the process. More often than not, they struggle with the language and the customs of their new homeland. RIF's founder, Maria Blacque-Belair, first appeared in the late summer of 2010. She lived near the flagship farm and stopped by one of our markets to introduce herself. Maria has a pyramid of reddish curls and wears the loose-fitting clothes cut from natural fibers of someone who has spent a lot of time in subequatorial climates. Her husky French-accented voice is unmistakable, and is most often heard proclaiming somebody's virtues as she introduces friends. Maria is never alone; she always arrives at the farm with someone in tow, whether a colleague from Doctors Without Borders, where she also works, or a playwright penning a piece about refugees being persecuted.

When we first met her, we were instantly won over by Maria's enthusiasm for her nascent organization. She had secured a bit of grant money with which she planned to provide stipends to refugee seekers as they trained in green industries, and was eager to bring her program's participants up to the farm to work alongside us. But more than learning how to farm the rooftops, she hoped that by partnering with us, the RIF interns would improve their English-language skills and become acclimated to their new home and its culture. So we agreed to try out a partnership, and the following spring, three bundled-up Africans arrived looking absolutely miserable in the forty-degree weather.

What we didn't know until later is the magnitude of the hardships many of the RIF interns had faced. Some had lost their entire families to civil war or genocide; others had been hunted by militias and feared for their lives even here; some of the women were victims of genital mutilation. Many were living in shelters as they awaited court hearings to determine their status here in the United States. That process can take months and sometimes years, especially when appeals are necessary, and during that period, our immigration laws prohibit refugee seekers from collecting wages or government assistance.

Over the course of that first season, we became quite close to the first class of RIF interns. Florence let Gwen practice her rusty French, and in exchange, Gwen helped her with her English. I gave Katy some Internet lessons, and Erick, who had been the executive director of a humanitarian-aid nonprofit in the Democratic Republic of Congo, became an all-star compost manager, flipping the pile with an ease that made it hard to believe he had been working since dawn delivering newspapers before arriving at the farm for the day.

Maria tells us all the time how valuable an experience the RIF project is for the participants in the Urban Farm Recovery Project. Sure, the farm offers RIF interns the opportunity to get some fresh air and engage in physical activity, which fights depression, and the teamwork helps those for whom English is a new language become conversational. But we undoubtedly learn more from our RIF trainees than the other way around. Erick would arrive each morning and greet everyone on the farm with a hug, which took some folks aback at first; but the gesture transcended basic cultural etiquette differences. When Erick arrived in the United States, he had no family or friends to hug. For him, the farm offered a sense of community that we took for granted, and his gratitude for these connections was a valuable reminder for us to appreciate the wonderful people who surround us and the fortuitousness of our own circumstances.

Since that first season, when we welcomed three RIF trainees at the farm, the program has grown in size and scope under the care of Matt Jefferson. His prior work with the Peace Corps resonated deeply with Maria's goals for the program, and the two began collaborating on ways to make it even more impactful. These days, the partnership has matured past its originally intended therapeutic purposes. We now teach some of the workshops in RIF's Asylum Support Seminars program. Gwen offered an introductory class on power tools, an incredibly useful skill set for entry-level carpentry or construction work, and I taught a class on how to apply for a food handler's certificate, which is often the difference between a minimum-wage food service job and a management position at a higher pay rate. Ben taught one on green jobs and another on cultural integration. One RIF graduate, Rodrigue, was accepted into a "Made in NY" job-placement program and is now a film production assistant. Téné obtained her food handler's certificate and is working on plans to begin commercial production of a delicious ginger drink using a traditional recipe from her native Burkina Faso.

When fifty-three-year-old Téné, who had spent twelve years being shuffled around the justice system in hopes of earning refugee status, finally saw her daughter again when she made the trip to her mother's adopted home of New York City, the farm was the first place she wanted to bring her. After traveling thousands of miles to a place where they don't know a soul, many of our RIF interns consider the farm the closest thing they have to a family.

Our relationships with RIF and City Growers add a social justice dimension to a business that doesn't have the latitude to dedicate resources to that crucial work. These are strategic partnerships in that our work makes theirs possible and theirs enriches ours in a way we couldn't accomplish on our own. But they wouldn't be on the roof—nor would we—if it weren't for another strategic partnership we work hard to maintain: that with nature. Farming is, at its core, a give-and-take with nature, a quid pro quo.

We've talked at length about the importance of fiscal sustainability, and how an enterprise can diversify its services and partner with other organizations to reach different members of a community, yet the very core of what we do—what all of this relies on—is simply finding harmony with nature. It's pretty basic stuff: a relationship based on a sentiment of "I won't mess with you if you don't mess with me." Take insects, for example: organic farmers talk about integrated pest management, or IPM, which is a low-impact approach to killing pests. Maybe you don't want to napalm your fields, because guess what? All those birds who live off the insects eating your crops will disappear when you decimate their food source, and then when those insects come back next season, this time in twice the numbers, you'll have to buy twice as much chemical pesticide to rid yourself of them, until eventually, they build up a resistance to that pesticide and you have to start over at square one. At that point, nature is basically saying, "You shouldn't have messed with me."

We've learned practices from the farmers who came before us that have helped us avoid these mistakes. In fact, we try to let nature handle nature whenever possible and just stay the hell out of it. For example, the first time we found a tomato hornworm, none of us had ever seen one before. There was some speculation that it might be a Luna moth caterpillar. Luna moths are gorgeous—and though they'll destroy your sweet gum and walnut trees, they aren't much interested in vegetables—so at first we were delighted. Then we watched as it began devouring our tomato plants before our very eyes, devouring an entire leaf in a matter of seconds. We all gasped in unison and plucked off the intruder before it could take down the whole row. To our utter horror, it reared up both its thorax and black, bumpy posterior horn (from which it derives its name), and spewed an alarming volume of green liquid. Everyone screamed. The thing was dispatched to the chickens immediately, who played a quick but intense bout of tug-of-war with it until the largest of them won and the others moved on to harass the bantam who had unearthed a grub that she was greedily trying to scarf down before her coop-mates could join the fray.

Consigning the creature to such a fate may seem cruel, but chemical-free pest management is a special kind of sadism. And we're fairly sure we're not alone in experiencing a certain kind of schadenfreude from witnessing the brutality of IPM techniques. On those days when the main valve on the irrigation breaks, the seeder keeps jamming, and it's so damn hot that every bed of arugula on the farm is bolting before you can get a second harvest, a farmer needs to feel like she's got control over *something*. And if that something is the population of aphids laying waste to the brassicae, then sorry, aphids, you're about to get sprayed with diluted peppermint Castile soap that will eat through the waxy coating on your bodies until you become desperately desiccated, ultimately frying in the sun.

Look, the truth is, we'd rather not take the time out of our day to strap on the backpack sprayer and walk the rows making sure every leaf is coated top to bottom in a soapy film that we'll have to take extra care to wash off at harvest time. We'd rather let our prolific population of ladybugs—who found their own way up without any help from us—wage war against the aphids in our stead. Have you ever watched a ladybug go to town on a meal of aphids? It's a thing of beauty. They can eat up to five thousand times their own body weight in those minute nitwits over their short lifetimes, and if we had less to do we'd probably just sit around all day watching them feast.

But we're too busy fighting the rooftop winds in a fruitless attempt at securing protective row cover over freshly sown beds to keep out the flea beetle colonies that make our greens look like a saloon door after a good old-fashioned shoot-out. Row cover is really the best way to beat these teensy jerks. It's a preventative method: you have to get a tight seal over the bed before the crop germinates, or those tenacious little shits will suss out their meal and destroy your harvest. Since we have such a low success rate with row cover, we don't have a great strategy for eradicating them, so flea beetles tie with whiteflies and aphids as the pests that cause the greatest amount of damage on the farm. Incidentally, they seem to find us earlier than most of their insect brethren, usually in the first season after installation

is complete, but their numbers typically drop as beneficial pred-
ator insects find the farm and catch up with them in subsequent
seasons. We also battle squash beetles, harlequin beetles, cab-
bage moths, and swallowtail caterpillars. We get help from all
the usual suspects, too: praying mantes chow down on the har-
lequins, dragonflies take down the occasional cricket, and perhaps our favorite are the parasitic wasps whose larvae we find
polka dotting those nasty hornworms. We always send an email
to our team at the beginning of hornworm season reminding
everyone to keep an eye out for the greedy pests, and attach two
photos: one of the healthy worms, with instructions to kill them
on sight, and another of their larvae-studded brethren, which
should be sent back out into the field to act as the Trojan horses
that they are.

Like any chemical-free farm, we abide by the tenet that
the best defense against pests is healthy soil, which makes for
healthy plants, which in turn are able to defend themselves
against pests and diseases more effectively. But if we can create
conditions favorable enough to entice a healthy population of
predatory insects, birds, and bats to call our farm their favorite
eatery, we are cutting down the amount of resources we have to
expend on fighting unnecessary battles.

We're forced to negotiate with nature every day in a highly
visible way, so we make the decisions we do—in favor of ecological health—because we can't turn a blind eye to the repercussions
of the alternatives. But the vast majority of businesses—whether

large or small, brick-and-mortar or digital—face the same choices that we do between messing with nature or trying to live in harmony with her. Except thanks to the way we've made the ecological degradation of this planet largely invisible to its inhabitants, most businesses don't have to think about it. They mess with nature, and they don't have to acknowledge the repercussions when she messes with them—and everyone else, too—right back. Maybe it's affecting an ecosystem far enough away so it's out of sight, or maybe the negative impacts of the business's practices are so slow to take hold that by the time they happen, we can no longer trace them back to the root cause. By now, we're all aware that the blithe attitude we've taken toward nature for the last century or two has been the least strategic movement in business history, ever.

Positive ecological practices support everyone on the planet. It's as simple as that: all boats rise with the tide. And that affects every single business's bottom line. If a clothing company is manufacturing shirts using cotton from fields drenched in pesticides, the physical health of the communities around those fields, not to mention the farmhands working those crops, will suffer. If the cotton is then dyed using synthetic chemical dyes that are illegally disposed of in our waterways, the ecological health of our rivers and oceans will suffer, depleting marine wildlife populations. If the workforce laboring over the manufacturing of those shirts is underpaid and confined to dangerous conditions, we create cycles of poverty that lead to famine, disease, and war. In the short term, we gain a cheap product, but ultimately, we pay the price. And ultimately, the manufacturer of those shirts will pay the price as well, when the land is no longer healthy enough to produce cotton, and the workforce that sews its hems is cut off by warlords taking advantage of a weak and impoverished community.

It's up to all of us to change the way we relate to the natural world. What we so often fail to see is how our relationships with resources engender or destroy our capacity to build community. The partnerships among ourselves will grow more competitive and contentious the more strapped we are for resources. As farmers, we are fortunate that our dealings with nature are pretty straightforward; we don't envy those who have to make hard decisions every day between short-term profitability and the health of the planet, especially when tens of thousands of jobs hang in the balance. But a triple-bottom-line business is sustainable in part because the extra money spent on environmentally gentle solutions will come back to a company in the way of community support, as soon as the community sees the extent to which the business has invested in its health.

If that argument is hard to swallow, we will say this: we love coming to work not because we make loads of money. We don't. We love it because we love the people, and we love the beauty of the ecosystem with which we've established a kind of symbiosis. Even the most misanthropic biophobe would have a hard time resisting the seduction of a beautiful day at Brooklyn Grange.

It's never the same two days in a row, but there's a bit of a rhythm: after a long morning harvest, worked in tandem, feeling satisfied, it's break time. A few folks mobilize and start pulling lunch together; there was an event last night, and the chef left a full tray of roasted beets in the fridge. Someone brings over half a bin of bruised tomatoes from the sorting station, a cucumber too gnarly and grizzled to sell, and a bunch of basil. Out comes the big silver salad bowl, and into it goes the pound or so of greens left over in the sink after washing the morning's harvest. Everyone's hands are lined with soil as they tear off chunks of pita from a pack in the middle of the table, using it to scoop some dip from a Tupperware, which they top liberally with our own hot sauce, greens, and chopped vegetables. Nobody cares about dirty hands here.

After lunch, two farmers use unplanted beds as pillows and nap in a row temporarily shaded by the adjacent skylight. Alton Ellis croons a rock-steady tune on the stereo propped up against the packing station under the water tower, and a breeze blows in from the river, drying the film of sunscreen and sweat on the team's dirt-freckled faces. It's just past noon, and we've been at it for six hours already. Across the farm, the chickens take languid dirt baths between meals of aphid-infested kale. Above us, two hawks swoop in graceful figure eights, like couples ice-skaters, and somebody points them out. All around, the bees hover, dropping down to dip in and out of blossoms like punch-drunk boxers. Everywhere on the roof, life ends, and life begins anew.

Epilogue

TOWARD A HEALTHIER BUSINESS ECOSYSTEM

When 2009 came to a close, we were well under way planning Brooklyn Grange. It had been an interesting year, fraught with anxiety. America had discovered just how much smoke and how many mirrors our economy was hiding behind. We had put one of our chief architects of financial fraud, Bernie Madoff, behind bars. Bitcoin emerged and presented the possibility of an economy without intermediary. Later, Arab Spring, and then Occupy Wall Street, would remind the world of the volume to which the populous voice could rise. The hacktivists behind Anonymous threatened the very instruments of power. We had voted a Black man into the highest office in our nation.

It was a time marked by potential. It was a moment during which revolution seemed possible. It was an interruption in the complacency of the status quo, a jolt reminding everyone of the fact that we are autonomous agents of our own fate. The word "disrupt" was chanted like an incantation. In the space that the skipped beat created, young, engaged minds everywhere sensed an opportunity to insert their voices and change the tune. Instead of overthrowing the systems, entrepreneurs were trying to change them from the inside out. Kickstarter, which launched in April 2009, gave creative individuals the opportunity to mobilize their personal networks in funding their projects. Uber (2009) and Airbnb (2008) lowered the barrier of professional entry for civilians to earn revenue through driving users around in their personal vehicles, and renting out lodging in their private homes, respectively. And the digital realm wasn't the only sphere that saw disruptive innovations grasping hold: the number of companies building tiny houses—minuscule dwellings selling for a fraction of the price of a standard-size home—rose exponentially, creating more accessible opportunities to become a homeowner. Coworking spaces gained traction, empowering individuals to conduct microentrepreneurial businesses without the high overhead of renting a dedicated office space.

The twelve months between the summer of 2014 and the summer of 2015, when this book was written, were a far cry from 2009. The economy was up, fuel prices were down, and people had jobs once again. The spirit of revolution had subsided. Yet in spite of relative prosperity, currents of unrest ran through the air. Race riots tore through the country, glaciers calved into the arctic, and a ridiculous number of candidates threw their hats in the ring to lead America into our next chapter. What happens next is anybody's guess.

Who knows if Brooklyn Grange would ever have received the support that it did—from investors, from the larger community, even from us, its founders—if there hadn't been such a spirit of transformation, a shift in public perception of what was and wasn't possible. Would we be successful in getting it off the ground in today's climate? In tomorrow's? Perhaps we were in the right place at the right time. Perhaps we would be doing our readers a disservice to advise that they, too, quit the jobs they've worked hard to get and follow their hearts toward an uncertain future.

We are determined to stand by the values that spurred us to launch, regardless of how the world around us has changed. Those values are firmly grounded in principles of triple-bottom-line business: doing right by the planet, and the people on it, while remaining profitable. We're not the only ones who follow these precepts. All the businesses we've mentioned in this book—the friends who supported us when we were starting out, the farmers who taught us much of what we know—they, too, are guided by the Three Ps. But what we've realized over the years, what wasn't as obvious to us when we were just starting out, is that it's the fourth P that matters most: partnerships.

The business world is an ecosystem, too. We feed one another, in our case, literally. We feed our customers, our restaurant accounts, the small mom-and-pop grocers at which we also shop. We support the nonprofit organizations that we house by providing the logistical framework for the enriching work they do. They, in turn, enrich our business and the lives of the many people they bring to it. They build rooms in the structure we create. The city provides economic stimulus, and in exchange, we provide green infrastructure that not only helps mitigate its environmental crises, but also provides amenities for its citizenry. We all support one another; we all work better because of our interconnections.

We are able to be a truly sustainable business because our partners shore up the areas of our operations that struggle and magnify the areas in which we shine—and we do the same for them. The NYC Department of Environmental Protection's green infrastructure program is interested primarily in ecological sustainability, particularly decreasing storm water management burden on the city's infrastructure. But by granting us the funds to install a green roof farm for a developer building housing for folks who might otherwise not be able to afford fresh, healthy foods, the DEP is now making it possible for all three of our organizations to offer a social return on a project that benefits each of us financially and protects our environment at the same time. The partnership does greater good than the sum of our parts.

An ecosystem is defined as "a group of interconnected elements, formed by the interaction of a community of organisms with their environment." That community of organisms can exert change on its environment. The stronger those interconnections are, the stronger an influence the community can exert. Tomorrow may bring a period of revolutionary change that gives rise to a new wave of enlightened entrepreneurialism, or it may bring a lazy and stultified lull that sees small shops get swallowed up by corporate giants. Regardless of what is happening culturally and politically when you start a business, the connections you form with the other individuals, organizations, and communities in your ecosystem will impact the future climate of that culture. In other words, if you have a dream but you don't think the world is ready, make the world ready.

When we first launched Brooklyn Grange, a lot of folks told us we were nuts. A lot of landlords simply wouldn't call us back. At the same time, a network of friends, strangers, and organizations helped to lift us up to where we are today. Now Brooklyn Grange is in talks with two different landlords about leasing a third roof. We're hatching plots to install solar arrays atop our farms and become more energy independent. We're increasing efficiencies, becoming more profitable, and continuing to grow our business. In a lot of ways, that means returning to our roots, refocusing on the priorities we set out for ourselves when we launched, the things that necessarily had to be put aside while we focused on staying afloat. We want to reexamine how our business can be a leader in social values. We want to give back to the community that brought us here.

That's a conversation we couldn't have had a few short years ago, when our only revenue was from vegetables and we were wondering whether we'd be able to pay ourselves enough to get by. But we are living in a very different world than we were five years ago. The world we live in today sees green space as a valuable asset, and hires us to build it in spaces public and private, small and large. The world we live in today has accepted our value, and in turn we have the latitude to ask ourselves how we can provide greater value to the world. When we started our business, we intended to find out whether it was possible to successfully operate a farm on a rooftop. As it turns out, a key part of contributing to the health of our business ecosystem is to never stop asking that question, and never stop evolving our definition of success. So as the seasons wane, and the plants on our rooftops begin to turn brown and die, we have a chance to catch our breath and look at our work. Our perennial self-evaluation presents an opportunity for new growth. And by the time the frost thaws in spring each season, we have planted new seeds for a stronger, greener, truly sustainable business.

ACKNOWLEDGMENTS

This book could not have been written without the thoughtful contributions of my partners. My name might be listed as the sole author, but the story and insights contained herein are all of ours, and I couldn't have told it without you. Gwen, thank you for taking the time to share your narrative with me over bagels and tacos. Ben, thank you for the countless hours spent reading, talking, and poring over soil tests. And, Chase, I can never thank you enough for being a sounding board and source of encouragement, and for always standing in my corner. Farmily, thanks for picking up the slack when I disappeared, and for the warm welcome when I reemerged.

To my agent, Rachel Stout at Dystel & Goderich, thank you for believing in this book. To my editor, Brooke Carey at Avery, thank you for your sharp eyes, close reads, and for never pulling punches. You helped me see the forest for the trees. To the team at Penguin: Anne, Caroline, Lindsay, Megan, and Roshe, thank you for helping us bring our story to the wider world, and, Justin, thank for helping us keep it local!

I owe a debt to several of our fellow farmers and green roofers. Molly Culver, thank you for your patient explanations of soil science, and for calling in the big guns. Zach Pickens, your thoughtful and frank analysis of urban agriculture should be shouted from the rooftops. Thanks to the Joes at Rooflite for your time and expertise! There should be a book written about your story. And, (soon to be doctor) Yoshiki Harada, you may not be a farmer, but you are quickly becoming as knowledgeable as anyone in the field.

My old boss, Joe Bastianich, the three years I spent learning how to be savvy by watching you operate has helped me every single day. Thanks for your support when it came time for me to fly the coop.

Alex, thank you for being a patient roommate and the best *hermana*, and for teaching me that impostor syndrome is normal. Aaron, thanks for the late-night brainstorm sessions on the roof. Mom and Dad, thanks for teaching me what real food is, and what to do with it. And, Neil, thank you for making sure I still got to eat some during the homestretch—you are a true partner and my best pal.

INDEX

INDEX